UP AT ALTITUDE

UP AT ALTITUDE

A Celebration of Life in the High Country

M. John Fayhee

JOHNSON BOOKS: BOULDER

This book is dedicated to my buddies Mark Fox and Michael Kirschbaum, who have politely listened to more of my bullshit in the past five years than anyone should ever have to listen to in their entire lives.

&

To the memory of Todd Freeze, who's now entertaining the masses up in heaven, and who is sorely missed by his many friends in Frisco, Colorado.

9 8 7 6 5 4 3 2 1

Cover design by Margaret Donharl

Library of Congress Cataloging-in-Publication Data
Fayhee, M. John, 1955–
Up at altitude : a celebration of life in the high country / M. John Fayhee
p. cm.
ISBN 1-55566-134-3
1. Outdoor life—Colorado—Anecdotes. 2. Colorado Description and travel—Anecdotes. I. Title.
GV191.42.C61-39 1994
796.5' 09788—dc20 94-42568
CIP

Printed in the United States by
Johnson Printing
1880 South 57th Court
Boulder, Colorado 80301

Contents

ACKNOWLEDGMENTS

I would really like to thank Bob Brown, publisher of the *Summit Daily News,* for graciously giving me permission to use material in this book that was previously published in that newspaper. I would also like to thank Bob for being the kind of publisher who would let the kind of stuff I write appear in his newspaper in the first place. As a token of my appreciation to the *Summit Daily News* and its parent company, Eagle-Summit Publishing, a portion of my royalties from the sale of this book will be given to the Friends of the Eagles Nest Wilderness in the name of Eagle-Summit Publishing.

Also, I would wholeheartedly like to thank the people of the High Country, especially those who, like me, call Summit County, Colorado, home. High Country dwellers are quick to tell a writer when something is good and even quicker to tell him when something sucks. I have learned a lot from the honesty of my neighbors up here in the High Country.

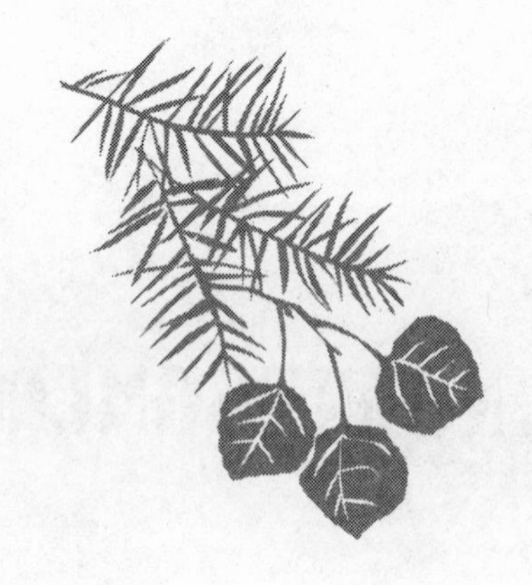

Introduction: Up

It is tempting to begin this book by saying something along the lines of "I fell in love with the High Country the moment I laid eyes on it—that the first time my boots ever tromped through High Country mud I knew that I had found my place on this planet and, no matter what sort of moneyless lifestyle crap I had to endure, I would never leave this place." You know, like David Quammen did with Montana and Ed Abbey did with the Sonoran Desert.

Well, vis-à-vis me and the High Country, such a statement would be an out-and-out lie, not that I have anything against including lies in my books, it's just that I usually prefer to hold back on egregious untruths until at least chapter two.

No, my first interaction with the High Country was not an especially pleasant one. I moved from Denver to Grand Lake, at the southwestern border of Rocky Mountain National Park, in 1983 and, almost from the get-go, I disliked the town almost as much as it disliked me. Like most married men, I am quick to say to my wife that the happiest day of my life was the day I was wed but, in truth, the happiest day in my life was the day I saw Grand Lake in my rearview mirror.

Over the years, I have come to understand that my negative relationship with Grand Lake and its negative relationship with me was just one of those things that can happen to any person in any small town anywhere, especially if both the town and the person-in-question are basically contrary by nature and opinionated by practice. That aside, it was several years before the thought of moving back to the High Country again entered my head. And, when it did (when I was offered a job with the *Summit Daily News* in Frisco, Colorado) I accepted the gig with a great deal of trepidation—to the degree that my wife stayed down in the lowlands for a few months before she moved up here with me.

Either I had changed or the High Country had changed. Whichever it was, I had hung my hat in Summit County, at an elevation of 9,100, for less than a week before I knew beyond the shadow of a reasonable doubt that I had indeed found my place. Even when I lived in Grand Lake, I always considered the High Country beautiful beyond belief. Its grandeur grabbed me by the heart. But, in places as in women, beauty only goes so far. Well, actually, it goes quite far; it just doesn't go far enough.

It took me a year or so of living back in the High Country before I came to understand just what it is I love about the High Country in general and Summit County in particular. And what I learned is this: the people who live up here at altitude are the best people in the world. They are people who dwell in some of the harshest weather conditions imaginable yet, by and large, they do so not only with a smile, but with vociferous enthusiasm.

This is a place where people burn the candle at both ends on a daily basis. People here work their asses off just to survive, yet they are professional recreators. High Country dwellers ski, hike, bike, paddle, run, practice martial arts, do yoga, take college classes, raise families, participate in plays, go to concerts, jump headlong into community activities, and get drunk with a degree of verve I have not witnessed anywhere else.

And they—we—do it in a place that is so rough it was never inhabited full-time until the 1860s, when the first crazy miners arrived on the scene. Up until then, several tribes of Native Americans roamed up here in the summer to hunt as well as a few beaver trappers in the 1840s, but, when the leaves started changing, they took their butts back down to the Great Plains posthaste. And it's not as if the Great Plains are climatically like the Bahamas or anything in the dead of winter.

These days, of course, the High Country, especially those parts of the High Country that are considered "resort communities" by state demographers (Summit County, along with Copper Mountain, Breckenridge, Keystone, and Arapahoe Basin, is the largest ski county in the country), is getting ridiculously civilized. We have Safeways, department stores, and espresso bars by the dozens. Our roads, which can easily see two or three hundred inches of snow a year, are plowed so thoroughly many High Country dwellers are starting to trade in their gnarly Toyota trucks, Jeeps, and Subarus for Volvos.

This advent of civilization, plus a palpable influx of people—especially those from California—who are looking not so much to live in the High Country as they are to get away from somewhere else, is causing this wonderful part of the world to change. Some of that change, like having some civilized amenities, is for the better. A lot of it, like having the average cost of a two-bedroom, cookie-cutter condo hovering somewhere around $120,000, is for the worse.

But, if a place cannot withstand a few changes for the worse, it's not worth its weight in snow or black ice. And I believe the culture of the High Country will endure and evolve its way through the myriad growth-related problems facing it.

After all, civilized amenities notwithstanding, it still takes cojones to live up here at altitude. In only a few places in the world do people live higher than they do in the central Rockies of Colorado (Nepal, Bolivia, Peru, et al.). In Summit County alone, we have two towns over 10,000 feet and three more over 9,000 feet. And, only a few other places in North America can lay claim to being bonafide "High Country," which, purely subjectively, starts somewhere about 7,500 feet. There are a couple of places in New Mexico, as well as one town in Arizona, that are over 8,000 feet.

Now, don't misunderstand me: I'm proud of this place and of living here, but I don't want to get into a pissing match with other folks who live in winter-dominated places. If you ever find yourself in the company of a Montanan or a Minnesotan, you know how easy it can be to fall into arguments that essentially amount to, "I'm more stupid than you, because I live in a place that's even colder than the High Country!"

The thing is, frigidity and serious snow are not the only things that make life up here hard. Whereas folks in parts of Montana and Minnesota surely suffer through harder winters than we do, their winters do not last as long as ours. (In 1993, we had a foot of snow on July 10.) And they do not have to deal with the physiological aspects of altitude. Humans were never designed to live up here. Once you pass the 7,000-foot level, the human body starts asking itself some serious questions about its own sanity. You dehydrate faster. Altitude sickness affects many of our visitors. You get drunk quicker. It's harder to bake cookies. All sorts of stuff.

What all this amounts to is: you should not come here under any circumstances, either to visit or to live. If you do come, you will likely observe that the High Country is populated by friendly folks who are by-and-large quite educated and well grounded. But your nose might start bleeding, and it might never stop. You may be dizzy from the moment you arrive until the moment your de-arrive. After one sip of beer, you may make a drunken fool out of yourself right in front of your mother-in-law.

It's simply terrible. You should go to Montana or Minnesota instead. There's more air, both of the hot and cold varieties, in both of those places.

What you should do is look upon this book as a substitute for either visiting or moving to the High Country. This book, I hope, amounts to a mosaic of what it's like to live up here at altitude. There is no continuity, just a hodge-podge of chapters that deal with some of the experiences I have had in the High Country, the people I have met, and the stories I have covered while working at the *Summit Daily News.*

One more thing: don't think for a moment that I am an expert in the subjects I write about in this book. Serious cyclists, for instance, will likely look at me as a dweeb when they read the chapter "Riding in the Courage Classic." All I can say to that is, "I might be a dweeb, but at least I'm a High Country-dwelling dweeb, which, as far as I can tell, is the best kind."

—On the banks of North Tenmile Creek, October 5, 1994

Experiences

Bear Tales on the Gore Range Trail

I am almost a little embarrassed that, after having lived in Summit County for four years, I had never hiked the length of the fifty-four-mile Gore Range Trail, which essentially connects Copper Mountain Resort with Green Mountain Reservoir. I've been on several sections of the Gore Range Trail, but had never taken the time to traverse the bugger end-to-end, which is generally the way I most enjoy getting to know trails. Many of my hiking companions feel I put too much stock in the concept of hiking properly named trails in their entirety in one fell swoop. They think I would do better to pay more attention to destinations than to particular trails. Well, on that I say "Screw 'em." I like long-distance hiking trails that boast specific names, and that is that.

For some weird reason, Summit County residents do not seem to have an intimate relationship with the Gore Range, despite the fact that it is one of the most splendid mountain ranges in the state. Most people who live here, even some of the more serious outdoorspeople, can recite mounds o' minutia about the Ten Mile, Mosquito, and Sawatch ranges, while the Gore Range, with the exception of a few trails (North Ten Mile, Meadow Creek, Lily Pad Lake) seems to remain pretty much unexplored by locals.

I understand that, as a whole, the Gore Range, which straddles the Summit/Eagle county border and which includes the 130,000-acre

Eagles Nest Wilderness, lacks a certain degree of sexiness because there are no 14,000-foot peaks within its boundaries. (The highest peak in the Gore is Mount Powell, 13,534 feet.) And, in Colorado, if a mountain range lacks fourteeners, then it is hardly considered even worth talking about, much less hiking in for more than, say, about an hour.

Before each summer begins, I establish my semi-annual "these are the things I will do in the next six months" list. Before the summer of 1993, I put at the top of that year's list: hike the damned Gore Range Trail, end-to-end. In August, photographer Mark Fox and I commenced to do just that. We were dropped off at the Wheeler Lakes Trailhead at Copper Mountain at about 8:15 AM, and we pointed our boots towards Green Mountain Reservoir. We planned to take four and one-half days to traverse those fifty-five miles, which is a leisurely pace by any body's standards.

As we cinched our packs, we couldn't help but notice that the temperature in the shade was hovering somewhere around twenty-five degrees. Our kind of weather. The last thing Mark and I want to experience during a mid-August hike is mid-August-like weather. Right.

Of course, the moment we started up the hill, which would basically continue for four-plus miles, all the way to Uneva Pass, we began to think that twenty-five degrees was a perfectly acceptable temperature option.

The Wheeler Lakes Trail, like most of the Gore Range trails that begin on Interstate 70, is impressively strenuous. It's not as tough a hump as, say, the Meadow Creek Trail, which starts in east Frisco. But, it'll do in a pinch, especially when you're loaded with five days worth of food and refreshment.

As the trail wound its way through the meadows and aspens, we caught up with a group of four dayhikers. These people were headed out on a long day's journey into the hills. They planned on hiking up to Uneva Pass, then down North Tenmile Creek, back into Frisco. All told, about six trail hours. That clearly is one of the cooler things about the hiking options in the Gore Range: there are more loop hikes to be had than Carter's got liver pills.

Each of the dayhikers looked to be in their sixties. And each of them was carrying a well-worn hiking stick, something you don't see much anymore. Time was when just about everyone who even stepped four inches into the woods did so with a hiking staff in-hand. As a matter of fact, you used to be able to tell a lot about a person you met on the trail by eye-balling his or her staff. Was it worn on the bottom? Was it shiny-smooth where the person held it? Did it look like it could tell you a few good yarns?

The use of hiking staffs is nowhere near as popular these days as it was, say, fifteen or twenty years ago. Hiking staffs have pretty much gone the way of clunker Vasque hiking boots, flannel shirts, and Sierra cups carried on one's belt. Hiking staffs, in the hyper-synthetic days of outdoors Here & Now, are sure signs of fuddy-duddy-dom. As such, just about the only people you see on the trail with hiking sticks any more are seniors, and I say that respectfully. For, you see, I am a hiking staff (I have always called them hiking or walking "sticks") devotee and toter from way back. Though I no longer carry my stick on short dayhikes (I used to), I still never backpack without one.

There is, of course, more to carrying a staff than simple practicality, though there is that. When you're traversing rough turf, especially when you're in the descent mode, and when you're crossing a particularly captivating stretch of river with expensive camera gear in your pack, hiking sticks are worth their weight in gold. Also, I have used staffs to deflect the nefarious intentions of more than one poisonous reptile and have found they are particularly handy when one has to make a quick exit from a less-than-friendly watering hole.

But, even a stick-lover such as yours truly has to admit that's about the end of line when it comes to hiking staff practicality. And, if the truth be told (and I am a stickler for stick-related truth), the worst on-trail injury I ever suffered was at the hands, so to speak, of a hiking stick. I was about two-thirds of the way through my five-month hike along the Appalachian Trail back in 1980, when, completely unexpectedly (which is the only way these kinds of things occur), my left foot slipped out from under me and moved briskly towards my right foot. All of my weight, and that of my pack (I had just resupplied in Hot Springs, North Carolina, the day before) came down big time on the point of my stick. Unfortunately, the part of my body that absorbed every iota of the impact was my left eye. My eyelid was almost completely ripped off, which did nothing to improve my already not-so-good looks.

Anyhow, clearly the concept, as well as the practice, of carrying a staff into the woods transcends, or at least ignores, practical considerations. It is foremost a matter of aesthetics and, admittedly, image. There's no doubt that image speaks to the "old days," which is something I used to generally avoid but find myself thinking more and more about as I move on towards the big 4-0. When it comes to carrying a stick into the woods, the old days seem like the right days.

After two miles, the trail branches. Take a right, and you end up at Wheeler Lakes, one of the most popular dayhike destinations in the county. As a matter of fact, the side trail to the lakes, which is only a few hundred yards off of the Gore Range Trail, is more prominent than the main trail. I must admit that this sort of thing is somewhat perplexing to me. Wheeler Lakes is one of the places in the Gore Range most likely to have about ninety to eleven people hanging out, even in the middle of the week. It's a nice enough spot, especially, I would guess, if you were here on vacation from someplace, like, say, Ohio.

But, all one has to do is head on up the trail a little further, and there are plenty of spots that are even more captivating, with far, far fewer people. Nothing against the company of my fellow human beings while I'm in the woods, mind you. But, the less, the merrier.

It took us about two hours to get to Lost Lake, another beauteous spot that sees a fair amount of visitation. But, that's okay, because just beyond the lake the trail passes from the trees and into the realm of the Sky Gods, Colorado-style—the alpine tundra. And, once you hit the tundra, the number of people you're apt to run into diminishes considerably. Certainly, thin air and lightning danger has much to do with that fact. But, I believe a lot of people simply take one look at the tundra and decide to hike back down. Treelessness makes many people feel psychologically exposed, like those dreams where you show up to your second-grade class sans garments.

As for me, I would rather spend time above tree line than in any other type of life zone on earth. This is not to shortchange high deserts, coastal mangrove ecosystems, or cloud forests. It is to say that, by way of a sloppy comparison, I never had any trouble understanding the late Edward Abbey's love of the Sonoran Desert because I have that same kind of love for the tundra. The main difference between Abbey and me in this context (besides the fact that he wrote books like *Desert Solitaire* and *The Monkey Wrench Gang*, while I write real estate stories for the *Summit Daily News*) is that he knew a lot about the Sonoran Desert. The sum total of my natural history-related knowledge of above-tree-line regions is that they are fun places to sit in the summer sun, sipping vodka-based beverages while reading a novel and smoking cigars (although I believe Abbey knew those kinds of things about his home turf, as well).

Ever since I first rubbed elbows with mountain tundra in 1979 while hiking in northern New England, it has been my fantasy to live within mellow walking distance of the world above the trees. And, though I am a rogue, a ne'er-do-well, and a poor planner who boasts an entire grain silo filled with negative personal karmic units, I have managed to pull that fantasy off. Sometimes, I can scarcely keep from giggling.

It is with springs to our steps that Mark and I hike the last few miles to Uneva Pass. I had never made it past Lost Lake before, so this was new territory for me—new territory located a mere twelve or so miles from where I hang my hat. Those few miles between Lost Lake and the pass were splendiferous. The Gore Range's tundra with its mists, flowers, talus slopes, and clusters of bristlecone pines is, by Colorado standards (which, in this context, are mighty high), at least a 7.5 on the Richter scale of jaws-agape appreciation.

Uneva Pass separates the Officer's Gulch and North Tenmile drainages. The trail makes its way around the head of a branch of North Tenmile Canyon—meaning it stays above tree line for an extra, extra long time. It passes by yet another lake, before dropping back down below tree line. All told, there is about a four-mile, toe-crunching descent before the trail intersects North Tenmile Trail. During this descent, a nagging leg injury (which was eventually diagnosed as bursitis located at the top of my iliac-tibial cluster) started nagging me badly. I tried to ignore it, but it would not ignore me.

We stopped for lunch at the junction of the Gore Range Trail and North Tenmile Creek Trail. I was one lazy piece of trash while I was buying my food for this hike. Usually, I am organized enough during the weeks preceding a hike to ask my wife to make me a whole buttload of her world famous granola bars. But this go-round, I either forgot to ask Gay to do just that, or I asked her, and she told me to get lost. So, for the next five lunches, I'll be staring down one tantalizing Power Bar and one mouth-watering Pemmican bar per day. Actually, I was thinking while we were sitting there next to North Tenmile Creek eating, that the Butterhorn Bakery is only about an hour's walk away, in downtown Frisco—so we could run into town, hoove a couple of quick deli sandwiches, and cruise on back to the trail. But, that would add another three hours or so to an already long day, so we dunked the idea.

I have never been a strong afternoon hiker. I especially loathe afternoon uphills. I would much rather knock off all the climbs and most of the mileage before lunch—which is what we had just done. With thirteen miles planned for the day, we had already hiked ten. Even though the walk from North Tenmile to Meadow Creek, where we planned to camp, was only three miles long with maybe a 1,000-foot climb, my carcass was pretty much dragging. It seemed like I was stopping to catch my wind about every one hundred feet. Mark was doing the same thing.

Though Mark and I are best friends, and though we have been in each other's company during a fair number of boneheaded misadventures, this trip marked the first time we had ever backpacked together, which is an incomprehensible thought. I easily remember a time when the notion of having an amigo with whom I did not backpack was impossible. I defined my friendships in the context of backpacking. I didn't give a hoot in hell if my compadres were psycho-killers with bad breath back in civilization, as long as they hiked well and were passable company out in the boonies. It was nice to be on the trail with Mark for another reason: my wife and I had just bought his pack for him, as a birthday gift. I have long and justifiably operated under the assumption that there are pretty much only two types of gifts in the world: those that pertain to the out-of-doors and those that aren't worth giving or receiving.

It took us almost two hours to finish the three miles between North Tenmile Creek and Meadow Creek. Since there was already one group camped near the trail junction, we moved downstream a ways. It was 3 PM, which, as far as I am concerned, is a perfect time to set up camp. It gives you plenty of time to put your tent up, bathe, change clothes, purify water and, most importantly, read and nap in the sun. I have always been perplexed by people who seem to be on the trail all day. Even while I was hiking the Appalachian Trail and the Colorado Trail, I would almost always be in camp by three.

Once again, I am pleased beyond description that I am not a photographer. Mark is carrying at least thirty pounds of camera gear, including two Nikon 8008 bodies, four lenses, a flash, about a billion rolls of film, two thousand filters, a mono-pod, and all manner of unidentifiable paraphernalia. I, on the other hand, am carrying my old (and small, light) Olympus XA, just so I'll have something handy to photograph Mark with when he dies of exhaustion from carrying all that weight up and down mountains.

More importantly, though, I'm glad I'm not a photographer because, when you're a photographer, you actually have to spend valuable relaxation time photographing stuff. As a word-scribbler, all I have to do is sit there on a log smoking a cigar while thinking deep thoughts, which I always write down later, because I can never be bothered to do so while I'm lounging around camp pondering the cosmos.

Dinner time finally arrives. For only the second time ever, I decided to go the freeze-dried dinner route. As I sit there trying to decide which provocative flavor I will dine on, I reflect that, at one time, I was considered a master of original, tasty, light, and filling backpacking dinners. Since I own a food dryer, I would customarily dry rice and vegetables, which I would then, on the trail, reconstitute and adorn with a wide array of spices. I have lost my momentum in that regard, and, as I stare down at a food bag filled with five freeze-dried dinner entrees, I promise myself to reestablish my culinary momentum the exact instant I return home.

Mark also brought freeze-dried dinners. Tonight he opts for a provocative rice concoction that bears a striking resemblance to the kind of industrial/biological sludge one sees on documentaries about waterways that are so polluted you're not even supposed to fly over them in a 747 at 30,000 feet, lest you develop some sort of oozing skin chancres.

It is my pleasure to dine on freeze-dried mashed potatoes with a turkey gravy that was so tantalizingly Thanksgiving-dinner-like I swore there for a moment that I was a central character in a Norman Rockwell holiday season portrait.

My wife was very curious to know what possessed me to procure (1) a freeze-dried dinner of any variety, and (2) a mashed potatoes with turkey gravy one under any circumstances. I have no excuses, though I must admit that I was proud of the quantity and quality of the intestinal distress I experienced as a result of this one skimpy meal. Mark was delighted that we each brought a tent.

After dinner, we had to deal with attempting to dance the two-step around what is becoming an increasingly bothersome ursine problem in the southern Gore Range. We had already walked far from camp to cook, as though any bear worth its weight in maimed human beings would be anything besides absolutely repulsed by the thought of eating the remains of our freeze-dried dinners. If anything, we would end up getting mauled because our dinner offerings were downright insulting to the local bear population.

Either way, we hiked over the ridge to Montana to do dishes. Then we went off in the opposite direction, down to New Mexico, to hang our chow. I had just purchased a brand-spanking-new food-hanging rope and was eager to use it. The new rope must have been charmed, because it only took me twenty-one attempts to get it over an appropriate-looking branch. The U.S. Forest Service recommends hanging your food at least eight feet off the ground and at least four feet out on a branch. In a spruce-dominated forest, that's not as easy as it sounds, because spruce branches were not designed with food-hanging in mind.

Because the mosquitoes were having their way with me, I went off to my little Sierra Designs tent by 8 PM, while Mark stayed up to, of all things, take pictures of the alpenglow off the Ten Mile Range.

I love crashing out in the middle of bear alert country. I am a big fan of bears, both black, which is the only kind we have here, brown, polar and, well, panda. I support the reintroduction of grizzlies into places like the San Juan Mountains of southwesternColorado, and I believe bear territory should be considered just that, bear territory.

There are basically two different kinds of outdoors people: those who have had sphincter-puckering experiences with bears, and those who have not. Now, it may well be argued, with mounds o' viability, that a sphincter-puckering experience with a lion, a tiger, or maybe even a bad-mooded buffalo ought to "count" in this context, which, when you get right down to it, is the context of BS-ing about the incident to your buddies when you're back in civilization.

There are even those who would carry that argument one step further, contending that your life-passing-before-you encounters of any variety—whether they take the form of stepping on a neotropical rattlesnake in the Central American jungles or almost falling off a cliff face because your protection was not being very protective—ought to, likewise, be justifiably included in the sphincter-puckering story club. Again, maybe so. Naw, definitely so. But, you've got to admit that the very word *"Bear!"*—especially when that word is being shouted in your direction in an extremely agitated tone-of-voice by someone in your immediate vicinity—is like no other. *"Bad-mooded buffalo!"* being screeched by your buddy while you're relaxing in the boonies is certainly cause to set down your vodka and Kool-Aid for a few moments. But, let's face it, it does not raise the hairs on your neck just thinking about it.

The equally, though decidedly different, fearsome yells, such as, say, *"Snake!"* or *"Brown recluse!"* are just not the same as *"Bear!"* because, though snakes and brown recluses can certainly lay their own unique brands of a world of hurt on you and yours, they aren't inclined, say nothing of able, to chow down on your corpus delecti piece by piece, and that puts bears in a whole different adrenaline category. Getting killed by something is one thing; getting eaten alive by something is a fearsome thought of a whole different color.

Like I said, my home county is fast becoming a bad news bear place. A buddy of mine was recently walking along the bike path near Frisco and, when he stepped in the woods to relieve himself, he was confronted by a bear scratching its posterior on a tree.

Another buddy of mine was awakened in the middle of the night by his dog barking. He heard something moving around out in his garage. He went out to investigate, thinking he would soon be dealing face-to-face with a burglar. Instead, he found himself toe-to-toe with a huge bear.

Then, a few weeks before our Gore Range Trail hike, a couple of Youth Conservation Corps kids were lying in their tent reading by the light of a candle, when suddenly they were joined by a bear who was apparently attracted by the candle's scent. Sad to report, that event occurred very close to where Mark and I were camping.

Summit County is, like the rest of Colorado, home only to black bears, which do not generally look upon you and me as lunch and dinner, respectively, as their cousins in ursine-ness, grizzlies, are sometimes wont to do. Nonetheless, black bears are (1) perfectly willing and able, under the right circumstances (which, unfortunately, the bears, themselves, define), to inflict serious physiological damage on members of our particular species, and (2) ofttimes big and ornery.

This, needless to say, is a wonderful combination of traits. Could you imagine living in a place where there is not at least some danger of being attacked by a wild critter that has the ability, to say nothing of the sometimes disposition, to rip your spleen out?

Not me. You take Delaware, if need be. I'll take bear country. Now, it's really important to stress that the chances of having physical harm laid on you by a bear in the Colorado High Country is remote. First of all, even though the numbers of bear-human "interactions" are increasing yearly, you are very unlikely to rub elbows with one of our ursine amigos, and second, even if you do, there will likely be nary a negative ramification from that encounter, as long as you don't do anything completely easterner-like idiotic, like run over and hug the bear, and/or the bear is not in some sort of foul, anti-human mood. Even if the latter point ends up being the case, this is not an attitude you can blame a wild creature for harboring, what with it being legal for our species to shoot and kill their species during hunting season and all.

Over the years, I've had the doo-doo scared out of me by bears on three occasions (though I have seen bears in the wild at least twenty times), and I wouldn't trade any of those experiences for a hot tub foray with the Swedish Bikini Team. After all, hot tubs with the Swedish Bikini Team happen in the High Country all the damned time. Close calls with bears happen only when your lucky stars are correctly aligned.

The first captivating bear experience I ever had happened while I was hiking the Appalachian Trail through the Great Smokies National

Park. It was about 6 AM, and I was dragging my not-quite-fully-awake carcass up Clingman's Dome, the highest point along the entire Appalachian Trail.

The foliage in those parts is thick and head-high. You wouldn't even be able to tell there was a trail unless you were standing right on it. The bear was not standing right on it. Rather, it was snoozing a few feet to the starboard of the trail. It was a fairly huge bear, as they all are when you run into them in the wild while you are by your lonesome. I literally came within about six inches of stepping on its foot. It jumped about nine feet in the air and let out with a powerful combination growl/scream at the exact same instant I jumped about nine feet in the air and let out with an equally powerful combination of a scream/scream. He went one way at full gallop; I went the other way at a dead sprint. We never saw one another again, though I would sorely love to run into him in a bar, just to see if he remembers me as vividly as I remember him.

Two days later, a buddy who was hiking with me and I were sitting in front of one of those chainlink-fence-enclosed shelters hikers are required to sleep in in the Smokies (because of the bear problems thereabouts). We were—how to say this tactfully? there is no way—stoned on our asses, and we were making popcorn, something that National Park Service literature tells you specifically not to do in bear country, because bears seem to really like popcorn, to the degree that the smell alone can drive them crazy.

We heard something coming through the thick underbrush, in a direction that we knew was trail-less. And it was assuredly something big. By the time we observed that huge black noggin peeking through the bushes, it was obvious that some serious, evasive action would be necessary *right damned now* if we were going to enjoy our popcorn without having a three-hundred-pound animal sitting in our laps, enjoying it with us.

That evasive action looked like something straight out of a Marx Brothers movie. We bumped into each other, dropped stuff all over the place, spilled stuff all over ourselves, and generally acted like people who should not be let out in the woods with or without strict adult supervision. We made it into the shelter and closed the gate behind us in the nick of time. Just as the gate latched, there was a big ol' bear tongue sticking through the chain-linkage, at perfect groin height, doing like a snake's tongue does when it's checking stuff out that it would love to bite.

Then, once while on a two-week solo hike in the middle of the massive Gila National Forest of New Mexico, I was walking down a creek in the early morning, pretty much minding my own business. At one point, the trail detoured away from the creek, around a thick stand of gambol oaks. About halfway by the oaks, I heard something move. I turned to investigate. *Bear!*

Fortunately, it was facing the other way, back in the direction I had just come from. I figured I could just slide on by without even being noticed. Sure enough, it disappeared upstream, into the oaks without laying eyes on my quivering self. As it disappeared, I considered myself lucky to have had an encounter with such a noble beast and all that nature-lover crap.

Then, it came charging out of the trees, directly towards me. The next seconds were the most vivid of my life. I quickly jerked the quick-release buckle of my hip strap open, dropped the pack and, in what seemed to my increasingly desperate mind like slow-motion, scampered through the woods and way up into a tree. The whole time I was making peace with my Maker, trying to talk my way out of a few recent indiscretions, asking that the branches of that tree be strong.

I never saw that bear again. Just as quickly, I forgot about all those promises I'd just made to heaven if I could just live another day. After about fifteen minutes, I warily climbed down. My legs were still shaking violently. With extreme discretion, I made my way back to my pack, which I was certain was mostly in the process of being digested by the bear. The pack was untouched.

More than likely, the bear had got a whiff of human as it was making its way upstream—the direction I had just come from. It probably turned and made tracks the other way. Only problem was, by that time, I was downstream. More than likely, after it saw me, it probably climbed a tree in abject terror, same as me.

The next few miles were strange. My adrenaline glands were working like a distillery, and I couldn't decide whether to run screaming all the way to the Gila Cliff Dwellings or to stroll coolly and cautiously. I chose the latter and lived to tell the tale.

Despite the fact that I have come away from my few bear encounters none the worse for wear, if I'm camping where there be bear, like in the middle of the Gore Range, I'm always going to be sleeping with one eye open. If a squirrel passes gas off in the woods somewhere, I'll come fast and fully awake, assuming, of course, that a little case of squirrel flatulence is, indeed, a one-thousand-pound monster grizzly with a bad toothache coming in through the side of my tent.

During the night, a squall blew in. The rest of the night was a mix of storms and bad storms, punctuated by the fact that, every time my rainfly contacted the side of my tent (which only happened about 200,000 times, because the wind was flat-out howling) I thought Bubba, the big bad bear, was bearing down on me.

It was still raining at 6 AM, which meant I had to sleep in, which certainly irritated me, because, as we all know, catching a little shut-eye while the rain pitter-patters off your tent is one seriously horrible way to spend time. Mark, who had set his tent up about fifty yards away, did not seem to be in an hurry to butt heads with the day, so hanging out in bed seemed like the right thing to do. We only planned to hike about twelve miles, so there was no reason to rub elbows with reality until the rains abated, which they did by seven.

A storm was seriously gearing up by the time we crossed Eccles Pass, a place I visit fairly often. By the time we got back to tree line in the Willow Creek drainage, it was raining like crazy. It was the first time I had seen the backside of Buffalo Mountain. Even though Buffalo looks relatively benign from the Frisco, Dillon, and Silverthorne vantage points, it is one rough-looking hombre from the other side. The Willow Creek drainage is one of the moistest places I've seen in Summit County. The undergrowth was almost tropically lush, and there were plenty of New England-like bogs.

There was also that increasingly bad pain in my leg. I had eaten a ton of Advil before hitting the trail. But it was obvious I should not be sashaying up and down mountains with a leg as tweaked as mine. Just as we got to an intriguing bend in the Gore Range Trail, where it intersects the Mesa Cortina Trail, I asked Mark if he would be too bummed if we blew off the rest of the hike. We had gone only twenty-three miles, and this would mark the first time I've ever dunked a hike in my life. I felt empty as we made our way over Mesa Cortina, towards the Silverthorne Wendy's. But—what the hell?—the rest of the Gore Range Trail isn't going anywhere. It will still be there, maybe even next weekend.

Riding the Courage Classic

Day One: The battle between self-doubt and cockiness rages between Breckenridge and Avon.

The Colorado High Country has to be the bicycling capital of the known universe. Whether you're talking about gnarly mountain bikers impudently ripping down a muddy backcountry trail, long-distance tourers limping along over 12,000-foot passes with near-terminal saddle sores, road racers dressed like extras in a grade-B 1950s sci-fi movie, or pudgy families of four from the flatland 'burbs white-leggedly moving along bike paths at the seemingly physically impossible rate of twelve inches per decade, the High Country often seems overwhelmed by people on bikes. On any summer weekend, when I eyeball the number of bikes on the highways and byways, I am reminded of *National Geographic* stories about hideously overpopulated places like Bangladesh, where tsunamis of people flood the landscape as far as the eye can see.

Some of the most poignant manifestations of this bicycling mania take the form of organized, charity-sponsored mega-tours. Every summer in Colorado, several of these kinds of tours hit our mountain highways. The two biggest, the week-long *Denver Post*-sponsored Ride the Rockies and the three-day Colorado Credit Union's Courage Classic (both of which raise money for charities), each draw well over two thousand riders, along with several hundred support personnel, dozens and dozens of support vehicles, and just as many police escort vehicles. These events, from a purely logistical standpoint, rival Exodus any day of the week. And, from a pure transportation perspective, Ride the Rockies and the Courage Classic are nightmares on every conceivable level, from people trying to simply drive down the damned highway on their way to work to RVers trying desperately to maintain their justifiable reputations as kings of the road when it comes to backing traffic up for forty-two miles.

Being a devotee of what planner-types call "dispersed recreation" (meaning, when it's playtime for yours truly, I prefer to get my butt as far away from the raging sea of humanity as possible), I have always been at least slightly perplexed about why people would choose to spend their limited R&R time on paved and often busy highways crowded with several thousand other people. Yeah, yeah, I know there's the "contributing to a good cause" stuff, but, hell, you can contribute to a good cause by simply pulling out your checkbook and mailing in some pecuniary resources. And, once that check is mailed, you can strap on your backpack and hit the woods, feeling mighty fine about your civic-mindedness.

But, I understand full well that not everyone agrees with that perspective, which, now that I think about it, is good, because it limits the numbers of people I run into in the woods while I'm dispersing my recreation.

For two straight years, the Courage Classic and Ride the Rockies both came through Summit County, with Ride the Rockies actually parking it for the night in Frisco both times it passed through these parts. Since towns that host mega-bike tours like Ride the Rockies and the Courage Classic always put on community-wide street parties, I have found myself rubbing elbows with about a gabillion Ride the Rockies and Courage Classic tour participants. They seemed like nice enough folks, and they seemed to be having a good enough time, even though, as a demographic group, I have always found road bikers to be a little lacking when it comes to their ability to consume mega-quantities of free beer—which really means nothing more than, after each of those town-sponsored bike tour parties, there were always several leftover kegs, a situation the residents of Summit County are usually well disposed to deal with constructively. Waste not, want not.

The thing is, every time I have attended a street party set up for one of these organized tours, I have felt like an outsider, because, well, I was. And, if there's one thing I hate, it's having a whole truckload of fun happening right in my very own backyard without interfacing positively with it.

So, in the summer of 1992, photographer/amigo Mark Fox and I decided to hop on the Courage Classic bike wagon. Riding in the Courage Classic seemed like, at best, such a good, noble idea and, at worst, like such a tame and innocuous notion when, back in February or March, Mark first asked if I would be interested in riding my bike, along with him, in this Courage Classic thing. (He thought it would be a good venue to meet women.) In order to participate, we would have to raise a minimum of $150 each in pledge money, which was okay, because the Courage Classic is set up as a fundraising enterprise for a bonafide good cause: Children's Hospital of Denver.

We sent in our forms and our registration fees—$35 each—while the High Country's winter winds were still blowing chilly and cold, and we were basically set. All we had to do was get in shape for a 160-plus-mile bike ride and raise that pledge money. But, hey, it was still the dead of winter; it was still ski season. We had half a year to get our ducks in a huddle, bike-wise.

Then, suddenly, time being the linear-moving thing it is, it was time to ride. Our bike-wise ducks were still decidedly unhuddled. Though we had talked a little about who we would contact regarding our needed pledge money, we had sorta neglected actually going through the process of contacting the people/entities we had talked about.

And, as far as the "getting physically prepared" part of our pre-tour preparations, we can honestly say they were not as bicycle-specific as maybe they should have been. If only the Moose Jaw Drinking Emporium and Pug Ryan's Bar (two of our eventual sponsors, I might add) had stationary bikes on-premises, we might have been a little more in-shape for this 160-mile bike ride.

This is not to say that Mark and I lead sedentary lives. It's just that bike riding, though pleasurable to both of us, is not the prime form of exercise for either of us. It is not even our tertiary form of exercise. But, hell, so what? The itinerary for the 1992 Courage Classic was, basically, right through the heart of our own backyard. The plan was to ride from Breckenridge to Avon the first day, from Avon to Leadville (after a loop around Turquoise Lake) the second day, and from Leadville to Breckenridge (after a loop around Lake Dillon) the third day. Surely, our basic familiarity with the local turf, combined with our extraordinary familiarity with all the best watering holes in the vicinity (for caloric replenishment, you understand), combined with the fact that we were both used to the high altitude would see us through the tour in a most manly way. Or, at least in a not-very-humiliating way.

Though the tour was not set to kick off until Friday, July 24, things were being set up early Thursday morning in Breckenridge's Carter Park. Mark and I showed up fairly early on Thursday to register. We were among the first to do so. That meant we would not have to go through the registration process Friday morning—at the same time two thousand other people were trying to do the same thing.

We met at my house at 6:30 Friday morning. Though we had already registered, we still had to drop our camping gear off. Like most of our fellow riders, we planned on camping out in Avon and Leadville, rather than renting hotel rooms. The Courage Classic people carry all your camping gear ahead for you in trucks, which is something I could get used to in a skinny minute. My wife drove us up to Carter Park, where we were promptly told we were in the wrong place. Good start. The luggage-carrying truck was down in one of the Breckenridge Ski Area parking lots. We went there, took care of getting our packs on the right vehicle and, quick as snails on Quaaludes, we jumped on our mountain bikes (both of us own Bridgestone MB5s with stock components) and hit the road.

At 7:15 in the High Country dead-of-summer morning, it is cold. We were both dressed in the height of summer fashion—if you live in, say, Mississippi. Our frigidity situation was exacerbated by the fact that the ride from Breck to Frisco is decidedly uncardiovascular. You have to touch your pedals about once every mile, and, even then, it's more to keep in practice than out of any need for additional momentum. Most of the riders seemed to prefer cruising this first stretch on the road. We preferred the bike path (which parallels the highway), if for no other reason than most of the other riders seemed to prefer the road.

By the time we got to Farmer's Korner, everyone was directed onto the bike path for the haul to Copper Mountain and Vail Pass. Right where the path heads into the woods from Farmer's Korner, there's about a six-foot-tall hill and, before we could say, "Red alert, initiate evasive maneuvers *now*," some not-so-skinny gentleman who was not-so-young and not-so-coordinated stopped dead in the middle of the path, causing dozens of brakes to lock up and many obscenities to be muttered. This man apologized profusely, saying how the little six-foot rise had caught him by surprise. We wondered how much of a surprise Tennessee Pass would be for this man the next morning.

At the west Frisco bike path parking lot, we enjoyed the first of what ended up being eleven "aid stations"—places where riders could stop and snack, drink, rest, and relieve themselves. Though it seemed a little early in the ride to be thinking in terms of chow, we stopped for a bagel—or maybe it was three bagels.

It was not long before those two thousand cyclists began spreading out—though, when you're talking about that many people pedaling along a twelve-foot-wide bike path, "spreading out" is a relative term. I had never in my life pedaled anywhere near that many cyclists. However, it wasn't as bad as it could have been. Because this was an organized event, there was a certain amount of esprit de corps-borne good manners. Usually, in my opinion, road bikers are not among the most mannerly of outdoor athletes. During the Courage Classic, though, there were polite requests to pass, and thank-yous expressed by those who were being politely told they were being passed.

I spent the entire way from Frisco to Copper talking to an older man who lives in Conifer who apparently rides in every organized tour held between here and Mars. He was on a light-looking, titanium-componented road bike, with tires about two nostril hairs wide. He would pedal about once every week. In order for me to keep up with him, my knees looked like the pistons in an oil viscosity TV commercial. Finally, I gave up and bid this man a fond adieu, telling him I would "catch up with him later." Right. All things being equal, there is simply no way a mountain bike can keep up with a road bike on pavement.

At Copper Mountain, there was yet another aid station. I had thought this ride would be a perfect opportunity to lose an ounce or two. Looks like a big negatory on that one. Though I once spent a summer touring on my bike from southern New Mexico up to Yellowstone, I must admit I know very little about the ways of road riders and/or tourers. I am quickly learning that calorie-loading is a large part of the cyclists operational strategy. Long-distance backpackers, who I am much more familiar with, chow several times a day, yes, but certainly not every half-hour, for Pete's sake. I may change my allegiances from backpacking to touring, if for no other reason than the opportunity to hoove every two seconds. As the frequency of these aid stations indicates, the process of organizing a huge bike tour like the Courage Classic is intricate and time consuming. Two people work full-time year-round to put this bugger together.

So, we've ridden about sixteen miles, and we've had two mini-meals and minimal sweat. Before us was the six-mile haul to Vail Pass. I've done this ride several times before, and I know it's a piece of cake. By the time Mark and I hit the summit, the clouds were moving in fast. It was about then I realized that my raingear was in the back of a truck somewhere, along with my tent and sleeping bag, heading to Avon. I was Gore-Tex-less at what ended up being a not-so-good time. I got soaked.

But, fortunately, it rained only enough to make certain that, somewhere along the line, I would have to ring my fashionable undies out. Then, the storm passed. The haul down the Vail side of Vail Pass, which I'd never done before, was one joyously heart-palpitating cruise. According to my brand-new Cateye cycle computer, I was topping out at about forty, which doesn't sound that fast, maybe, but my truck will barely go any faster. At the bottom of the hill, there was no aid station. Rather, there was a full-fledged lunch station.

Up until the lunch stop, I had thought Mark and I were fairly far up front in the pack. We weren't. There were at least five hundred people at the lunch site when we arrived. Soon after we sat down to eat (turkey and ham sandwiches and potato salad and cookies and some other stuff I forget), we heard one of the tour volunteers say the first riders had arrived in Avon at 9:15, an hour and fifteen minutes ago.

The ride the rest of the way to Avon was delightfully uneventful, except for the fact that we pulled into the Hubcap Brewery Pub in Vail thirty minutes before they opened for the day. This does not happen to us often. We'll usually find ourselves knocking, thirsty-like, on a bar door thirty minutes *after* closing time. Time of day aside, it's still the same kind of feeling.

I have never been able to force myself to like Vail. Even though Eagle County, where Vail is located, and Summit County border each other, the two places could not be more dissimilar. Vail has a very justified reputation for the kind of snootiness that often accompanies extreme affluence, which is okay, except for the fact that, in Vail's case, that snootiness has managed to trickle all the way down to the working class. Vail is the only town in Colorado where one finds arrogant twenty-three-year-old Village Inn waitresses and pretentious gas station employees.

One thing I will grant Vail, though: When it comes to Colorado's ersatz ski towns—the ones that were built from scratch where, before, there was essentially nothing—Vail tops the list, aesthetically. Keystone Village and Copper Mountain, also ersatz resorts, cannot hold a candle, ambiance-wise, to Vail Village. There are even times, usually around Christmas, when it's snowing big ol' flakes and people are in the holiday spirit, when Vail almost seems human, its aforesaid reputation notwithstanding. It almost feels like you're in a real town, with real people, who just happen to be wearing $1,000 worth of aprés-ski clothing.

Neither of us was even slightly fatigued when we arrived at Nottingham Park in Avon. The gear truck was not there yet, so we moseyed on over to Cassidy's for a beverage or two. On the way, we passed, just an instant after it happened, a bike-to-bike head-on collision between a tour rider and a non-tour rider. For only the second time since I became a Medical First Responder, I actually had the chance to first respond to some folks. I was psyched.

I quickly did a little visual triage and ran up to the poor schmuck who seemed to be in the highest degree of a world of hurt. As per protocol, I introduced myself as a First Responder and asked if I had his permission to treat him. This guy, who was an Avon local just out for an afternoon's bike ride, had a nine-mile, L-shaped gash on his forehead that was head-bone-deep, and he was walking around in circles, moaning mightily. (The other guy, the tour rider, was lying on the ground, moaning, which I thought was a little sissy-ish, since he only had a seven-mile gash on his head.)

Ended up that my patient was a native of Peru and the twelve or fourteen words of English he understood did not include "First Responder." This was fast getting better. Not only a chance to actually treat someone but, concurrently, a chance to speak a little Español. Before I could say "Que paso?" though, paramedics were on the scene and I was relieved of my lifesaving, Spanish-speaking duties.

By the time we returned to Nottingham Park, slightly more "relaxed," from Cassidy's, the gear truck had arrived. The ball field that was the official Courage Classic camping place was already a sea of tents. We managed to find spots on the infield, over near first base, tantalizingly close to the railroad tracks, which railed most of the night.

One of the local athletic clubs was offering free showers to Courage Classic riders, and Mark took advantage of that situation. I punted, feeling that, after only a day on the road, I was not yet sufficiently stinky to merit a shower. And, besides, riding in the downpour that nailed us near Vail Pass had de-funkied me as much as I needed to be de-funkied. Instead of showering, I rode back into town for some pizza—not having eaten in several minutes. As soon as I arrived at the restaurant, an afternoon-long thunderstorm moved in. Thus, I found myself trapped without recourse in a watering hole for three hours before the deluge let up even slightly. In the meantime, sad to say, my liver was deluged and, well, already the overall quality of the next day's ride was set in stone.

And, unfortunately, that stone was very large and, sometime during the night, in between trains passing by, some mean person beat me repeatedly on the head with it.

Day Two: The battle between Tennessee Pass and my head rages between Avon and Leadville.

When we first signed up for the Courage Classic, we were given a choice of "meal plan" or "no meal plan." Mark chose the former; I chose the latter, mainly because every single group meal in history has had, in large quantities, onions as a main ingredient, and I would rather rip my own teeth out with pliers than consume even one molecule of anything that has even been in the same room as a damned onion.

When we arose at dawn on Saturday morning, I found myself badly in need of coffee, ice water, and the biggest, greasiest breakfast this side of a street vendor in Juarez. (Those of you who may have, at one time or another, consumed rather too much beer in one day know what I'm talking about here.) Mark decided to bypass the group breakfast and ride with me the eight miles to Minturn, where the Turntable Restaurant is thank-god-fully located.

While at the Turntable, Mark, being conscious of the fact that we were about to ascend Battle Mountain and, immediately thereafter, Tennessee Pass, opted for the fruit plate. I, being unconscious on all levels, opted for a monster stack of pancakes, with extra butter and syrup and a double side of sausage. When I am suffering from near-terminal bottle flu, there's nothing I crave more than a plateful of grease. If I could have figured out a way to rig an intravenous set-up on my handlebars, I would have, and I would have filled the bottle to the top with bacon drippings.

That mound o' chow seemingly worked a miracle of near biblical proportions. I was a new man, and Mark and I attacked Battle Mountain with vim, vigor, and verve. Okay, maybe we didn't exactly attack it, and maybe our vim, vigor, and verve quotients were a little lacking, but at least we didn't run from it, screaming in falsetto voices.

Much to our surprise, we passed almost as many people on the way up Battle Mountain as passed us. The main reason we were surprised we actually passed anyone was the fact that we were on mountain bikes, while most of our Courage Classic compadres were riding road bikes. I even had several people in Avon the night before comment on how stupid it was to be riding a mountain bike on a road tour. Well, I politely informed them, since I am not exactly the world's most affluent person, given a choice between the two major genera of bikes, I preferred owning a mountain bike, mainly because of its versatility. One can ride a mountain bike on a paved road, but one cannot ride a road bike on some nasty-assed single track through the middle of the mountainous woods. So there.

Unfortunately, because mountain bikes are a lot heavier than road bikes, and because mountain bike tires tend to be knobby and wide rather than smooth and microscopically thin, it's literally twice as hard to make a headway on a paved road while riding a mountain bike. So, even though we passed a fair number of folks, which was cause for some degree of reserved bravado, we were just as often passed by fat people wearing thongs and Bermudas riding rusty three-speeds with kick-stands limply hanging off the side and getting clack-clacked by the peddles every point-two seconds—which was not cause for *any* degree of bravado.

It was along about here that I really started scrutinizing the gear that these serious bike people sport. In the outdoor equipment pantheon, cyclists, at least by reputation, are without peers. If there is one outdoor-gear-buying demographic group that jumps on every new technological upgrade like flies jump on cowpies, it's cyclists. Backpackers, climbers, and downhill skiers are not exactly innocent when it comes to coveting the latest sport-specific gizmos and gear. But, compared to cyclists, backpackers, climbers, and downhill skiers go about their recreational equipment-procuring pursuits with a near-monastic degree of gearlessness.

After riding in the Courage Classic and listening to about a zillion cyclists talking about bike gear, I concluded that someone could invent a battery-powered, $500, cross-bar-mounted crotch fan, and it would sell like hotcakes. I mean, these people are obsessed about this gear and clothing thing. I talked to several riders who had upwards of $2,500 invested in their bikes. And a couple people's bikes were in the $5,000 class. (Mine cost $350.) I overheard several conversations wherein people said they just dumped upwards of $200 on *new titanium wheel skewers,* which save something like two ounces of weight, compared to non-titanium wheel skewers. A wheel skewer could be filled with pure cocaine while simultaneously containing a few drops of a secret formula that, when ingested, would make me look like Mel Gibson, and I still would not pay $200 for it.

Up until we were about a mile from the Tennessee Pass summit, I was actually cruising fairly strongly, my hangover notwithstanding. Then, I hit the wall. Or, more accurately, the wall hit me. It took a month to finish that last mile. At the top, there was (of course) an aid station. I staggered over to the food table and, to this very day, the volunteers gathered there are talking, with quiet awe in their voices, about what I did to their Fig Newton supply. Then, replenished, but still a little on the queasy side, I pulled out towards Leadville.

At least in theory, any time you ascend a pass, you're supposed to be rewarded with a downhill screamer of a duration that at least closely approximates the hill you just dragged yourself up. Not so with the "descent" from Tennessee Pass into Leadville. Because Leadville is located at 10,200 feet above sea level (it is the second-highest incorporated town in North America, after Alma), it was sort of a disappointing ride down.

At least I was able to finally set my own pace on the ride from Tennessee Pass to Leadville. Up until then and there, I had to constantly adjust my cadence to account for other riders. By the time we topped Tennessee Pass, those two thousand Courage Classic riders were sufficiently spread out enough so that I finally felt like I could breathe.

The Courage Classic powers that be had decided, when they set up today's route, that a direct path from Avon to Leadville would not be courageous enough for the riders. The instant we hit the Leadville city limits, we were routed right back out of town, towards Turquoise Lake. I had never been on the road we rode. It was one seriously wonderful piece of pavement. Concurrently, it was one serious testicle-buster. After about three miles of mostly uphill, it was time for lunch. Both Mark and I were famished, so we grunted big time while sitting overlooking the lake.

Once back in the saddle, we realized it would have been better if we had fasted. On every Courage Classic itinerary, there is always one hill that is dubbed, for the duration of the tour, "Courage Hill." Our Courage Hill began its climb to the upper atmosphere almost immediately past the lunch spot. This was one attention-grabbing stretch of road. With each down-shifting, my lunch was upshifting. Much as I like turkey sandwiches, I prefer to taste each one only once. Finally, many years after civilization as we know it collapsed, we topped out. Unlike the Tennessee Pass scene, this climb ended with the kind of raucous downhill G-force-manufacturing descent one comes to expect from the Rockies. Our cheeks were pulled back and our eyeballs were being smooshed inside our grinning heads.

The rest of the ride to Lake County High School, where all Courage Classic campers were camping, was one uphill/downhill combination after another. After fifty-eight or so miles, we just beat out one of the hardest rains of the summer. An hour or so after we pitched our tents on the high school lawn, Noah floated by, looking bemusedly at our dripping bikes, like he was wondering why he did not have two of them on board.

It basically rained off and on all evening and all night. During a rare rain respite, Mark and I walked into town for supper. When I first moved to Colorado in 1982, Leadville really rubbed me the wrong way. Back then, it was still a working mining town that registered 9.9 on the Richter scale of redneckness. Leadville plain and simple used to feel like one mean little town.

Since then, all the local mines have closed, and Leadville has had to jump on the tourism bandwagon. Thus, it has necessarily moved towards a modicum of civility and couth. Leadville's downtown, which is one of the state's prettiest, has seen ample renovation work. And, more and more, Leadville is evolving into a bedroom community for Summit and Eagle counties, meaning there are more people than ever living in Leadville whom I might actually have something in common with. I, myself, have come to like Leadville enough that I once asked my wife if she would consider moving over there, if for no other reason than home prices are literally half what they are in Summit County. (Affordable housing is not the only reason I would like to live in Leadville. The state's two highest peaks, Mount Elbert and Mount Massive, dominate Leadville's skyline, and two wilderness areas, Holy Cross and Mount Massive, are located a stone's throw from the town limits. Those are *good things.*)

She told me, in no uncertain terms that, if I thought she was going to move to a town not only higher than Frisco, but 1,100 feet higher than Frisco, then I was even stupider than she already thought I was, which is saying a mouthful. She said I was perfectly welcome to move to Leadville, but I would be looking for a new wife if I did. I thought about it for a few beers and decided that, as long as it took me to find my first wife, I had better drop the notion of moving to Leadville.

I mentioned earlier that Leadville is the second-highest incorporated town in the state and thus, the country, and thus, the continent. There is, not surprisingly, a story behind that reality. Altitude has always been a source of pride to High Country dwellers. Many states include populations on their town limit signs. Some states include incorporation dates. In Colorado, our town limit signs include elevations. Up until the winter of 1993–94, we had a neat little system here in Colorado. We had a legal designation between towns and cities. Towns were incorporated entities that had populations below whatever number it was, while cities were incorporated entities with populations above that number.

Thus, Alma, at 10,300 feet above sea level, was the state's highest town, while Leadville was the state's highest city. And everyone seemed happy. But, for reasons that have much more to do with the overall quality of the Colorado State Legislature than they do with logic, the town/city designation was dunked. So, the fight was on between Leadville and Alma. When Leadville was referred to in some newspaper story as the highest town in the country, Alma's civic pride was bruised.

There were arguments about where town elevation measurements ought to be made. Traditionally, those measurements have been taken at a town's town hall, but there was no law or anything so stipulating. So, Leadville and Alma each started looking for points in town that were higher than their town hall elevations. Alma even talked about annexing 14,000-foot Mount Democrat. This went back and forth for a few weeks, until Alma finally came out on top. Leadville tossed in the towel and has been licking its altitude wounds ever since.

Day Three: The battle between wanting to ride over Swan Mountain and wanting to go home and watch the Olympics rages between Leadville and Breckenridge.

Before this trip began, I found myself debating the vagaries of Fremont Pass with one of the ladies I work with at the *Summit Daily News.* It was my contention that the ride from Leadville to Fremont's summit would not be too hard. This woman told me I was an idiot. And, since she had ridden it and I had not, and since she was a studly rider and I was not, I spent a lot of that night and the next morning in a ride-oriented reflective mood.

It was not the best of nights to begin with. I love camping perhaps more than anyone I have ever met. And I have spent more nights in tents than just about anyone I know. My idea of camping, and my attraction to sleeping in a tent, though, has a lot to do with spending the night in a remote area with as few members of my species in the general vicinity as possible.

In Leadville, my tent was set up exactly one foot from Mark's tent, which, in turn, was set up one foot from Lake County High School's main driveway. I had a total of five tents all around me, and all of them were close enough that methane releases were easily audible from tent to tent. Getting out in the middle of the night to relieve oneself required a combination of very good aim and an aggressive repression of childish instincts.

This was a good time to ponder on the camping differences between cyclists and backpackers. I have always been amazed at how sloppily bike tourers camp. I once almost got in a fistfight over this subject with a guy who was riding the Bike Centennial route from coast to coast. The only reason the conversation did not degenerate to blows was, while I was calling this guy a camping putz, and while he was calling me a backpacking elitist, his stove, which was right behind him and upon which his dinner was cooking, blew a gasket because he had both overpressurized it and set it up incorrectly. It caught on fire right then and there, and, as this guy entered a stuttering rage trying to rectify a clearly nonrectifiable situation that was exacerbated by the fact that I was, during this whole time, rolling on the ground at his feet, laughing my fool head off, I made a mental note that this could clearly be classified as an argument won. (I later shared my dinner with this guy.)

It was one thing to see the general amateur quality of the tents pitched all around me in Leadville, because, as I said earlier, cyclists seem to be focused on procuring, not surprisingly, top-of-the-line biking gear, rather than even mediocre camping gear. What really caught my eye, though, was how poorly these people were setting their tents up. With a gnarly thunderstorm fast approaching, it was obvious that the vast majority of my fellow riders would be sleeping the night away on water beds.

Mark and I ate breakfast in Leadville and hit the road by 7:30 AM. At the base of Fremont Pass—surprise of surprises—there was an aid station, and we both took advantage of it. Then it was off, in serious business-like moods, to the pass. It ended up being a remarkably benign ascent. On top, people were hugging and congratulating each other, talking about how it was all downhill to Breckenridge. Knowing that we were being routed over Swan Mountain Road, which I ride often, I decided to keep mirthfully silent.

It was one pleasant downhill all the way to Frisco, where I live. As a matter of fact, we passed within a half-block of my dwelling and, right there, on the other side of the front door of the Casita de Fayhee, was my TV set, with the Barcelona Olympics going full tilt. Mark and I had casually chatted about blowing off the rest of the ride when we got to Frisco. Since we both knew the around-the-Lake-Dillon loop well, it seemed a trifle silly to join the crowd for an extra eighteen miles that would present nothing new in the way of visual stimulation.

Besides, we were both starting to get a little burned out on the ride (i.e., our posteriors were killing us). But, since both of us played high school football and were, thus, at an early age, indoctrinated with the concept of seeing projects through, no matter how much your inner being was crying for you to do otherwise, lest you be ridiculed in public by people you wish to kill, we proceeded towards the lake.

Frisco was virtually saturated with bikes. Not only were the Courage Classic riders in town but, at the same time, so were the Frisco Criterium riders. It was nuts, and the Frisco Police Department was clearly having a tough time keeping cyclists and car-ists from killing one another. There was much in the way of name-calling and middle-finger-extending. It took a long time to get out of town and out onto the Dillon Dam Road. Once we passed Dillon, riders were given the choice of heading straight over Swan Mountain Road or taking a side trip to Loveland Pass. The Loveland Pass alternative gave people the opportunity to add a "century" (one-hundred-mile day) to their resumes. We passed on the pass.

Swan Mountain caught most of the riders with their skin-tight pants down. One lady snarled something to me like, "I thought all the uphill was done!"—like I personally (1) had something to do with route selection and (2) designed and manufactured this here hill. I told her not to worry, that this climb was only eighteen miles long.

From Sapphire Point, where the very last aid station of the tour was located, to Breckenridge was the very definition of a cake walk. Or a cake ride. Before we knew it, we were back, along with most of our two thousand compadres, in Carter Park.

Like every rider, we were cheered by people who obviously knew nothing about our backgrounds. They handed us medals and ushered us towards the free food. There was, to our dismay, no beer. But, we were confident we could survive. After all, hadn't we already tackled Courage Hill without retching? Damn right.

Winter Camping

For the vast majority of us, even those who count ourselves as members in good stead of the loyal order of "fanatic campers," winter in the High Country is very definitely the off-season. About the time the first snows fall, and usually about the time the first leaves fall, sleeping bags, tents, stoves, water bags, Therm-a-Rest pads, cook-kits, water filters, plastic coffee cups with grotesque stains, and backpacks get stuffed far away in the darkest recesses of your least-used closet until the season of snow leaves the High Country for that annually occurring six or eight seconds we know as "summer."

With the exception of professionals like Outward Bound instructors and their ilk, I have met only a few people in my entire life who have spent more nights in tents than yours truly. Yet, in a camping/backpacking career that has spanned almost thirty years, twenty or so countries, and thousands of trail miles, I have always defined "winter camping" as "camping in Central America in January."

One of my oldest buddies, whom I have camped with more times than I can, or care to, remember, moved years ago to Washington State specifically because he likes camping in the snow so much. He has always been absolutely nonplussed by my aggressive lack of enthusiasm regarding winter camping, especially when he contemplates where it is I live. He has told me many times over the years that he would a million times rather camp in ninety feet of snow when it's ninety below than he would in the middle of summer when the flowers are blooming, the birds are tweeting, and the temperature is hovering noticeably above the terminal frostbite level.

Part of my buddy's enthusiasm for winter camping is subjectively aesthetic. Though he thinks the Cascades are extremely beautiful under any seasonal circumstances, he just happens to think they are most attractive when they are under a blanket of snow. And part of his enthusiasm is based upon more objective factors. He likes the fact that wintertime bugs are few and far between, as are wintertime hordes of dorky humanoids. Though those factors have always seemed, from my personal sidelines, to be valid, they have, in my mind, always been mitigated by four equally valid counter-factors.

First is the frigidity situation. When one camps in the dead of winter in winter-dominated places, it is sometimes not so hot. And this not-so-hotness can and usually does have, at a minimum, serious ramifications when it comes to comfort, or lack thereof.

Second is the length-of-day problem. Though some of the happiest hours of my life have been spent in tents, I generally get a little weary of lying on the ground after thirteen or fourteen straight hours, which is how long it's dark in the winter.

Third, there are the realities of gear, which has two sub-counter-factors: (1) If I ever got into winter camping, I would have to either buy, rent, or heist a whole bunch of winter-camping-specific stuff, which would cut into my bar-hopping budget; and (2) all that extra stuff would weigh a gazillion extra pounds.

Fourth, and most importantly, there are avalanches. To some people, it's snakes. To some it's spiders. To some it's heights. To some it's mothers-in-law. To me it's avalanches. I know for a fact that, when I venture forth to meet the Fayhee Buddha, it will be via the avalanche route, and it is my life's goal to put that off for as long as possible. Call me a wuss.

But, I must admit, over the years, I have found myself attracted more and more to the notion of winter camping, if for no other reason than I am addicted to spending fairly long periods of time in the boondocks. My ability to handle workaday life is directly proportional to the time I am able to spend away from workaday life. Six-month-long annual noncamping, cold-turkey sessions are getting harder and harder to take, the older I get. Though I can placate my psyche in this context by making frequent day-long forays into the backcountry via skis and/or snowshoes, I sorely miss dozing off and waking up in a tent. That is as much a part of me as my name.

One winter, I finally bit the bullet and decided to try some U.S. grade-A bonafide winter camping. My guide for this undertaking was Josh Elmore, one of the owners of the Adventure Source in Breckenridge. Like all of the folks who own and operate the Adventure Source (and there seem to be many), Josh has considerable experience tromping through the backcountry in all seasons, including winter.

Josh had invited photographer Mark Fox and myself to join him and Adventure Source co-owner David Lawson (who would actually arrive in camp several hours after us) on a simple one-nighter on the side of Mount Baldy, a prominent peak on the Continental Divide. The plan was to snowshoe in only a few miles, set up camp and hang out drinking schnapps until it was time to hit the sack. Then we would sleep, get up, pack up, and head back to town. All in all, a very good plan for a couple of winter camping neophytes such as Mark and myself.

We left on a Monday afternoon, and it was remarkably hot and sunny. We literally could have hit the trail in shorts. We strapped on the Tubb's aluminum snowshoes Josh supplied us with and began our ascent to tree line. Many people consider "walking" and "snowshoeing" to be more or less synonyms. As in: "We walked up the trail while wearing snowshoes." This is wrong. Snowshoeing is a completely different animal. As in: "We stumbled, slipped, and slid our way up the trail like the lummoxes from hell while wearing snowshoes." Of course, Josh seemed to have a better handle (by, like, one-hundred-fold) on this awkward form of alleged perambulation than either Mark or I. This is not to say snowshoeing requires anywhere near the degree of technical expertise one needs to not crash and burn while skiing. It is to say that, while wearing a forty-five-pound pack, snowshoeing requires a completely different understanding of both physics and physiology to successfully make headway up the side of a mountain. Picture the way you would cruise on-foot if you were constipated for, say, twelve weeks, and you have a basic understanding of snowshoeing technique.

The alternative, though, is to not wear snowshoes, upon which case you would be digging snow out of your underwear as you stood there immobile, waist deep in the virgin powder with a very stupid look on your increasingly hypothermic face.

The snowshoe in to camp was all uphill, though we only gained a few hundred feet. We found ourselves actually sweating like twelve pigs and seeking out shade whenever we stopped to catch our breath, which happened often.

Josh already had an idea where he wanted to camp. When we arrived there, he pointed us to a slope that, in the summer, would hover somewhere in the 30-degree not-level range. But, with deep snow on the ground, all you have to do to make a level spot is pull out your shovel, which Mark so nicely had carried in for us, and dig out a few hundred tons of heavy wet, you guessed it, snow. When you have a spot dug out that's big enough to hold a tent, you commence to building a wind wall around where the tent will go. Josh's wind wall ends up looking like a well-sculpted foundation of an igloo. Ours ends up looking like something Calvin and Hobbes would build on a bad day. Josh endears himself to us by not laughing directly in our faces at our incompetence.

Once the two Sierra Designs Stretch Preludes (weighing in at almost ten pounds each) are up, we are essentially done for the day. It is 3:30. Time to relax. Relaxing around camp is definitely one of those things that's done differently in the winter than in the summer. In the summer, you'd pull up a sitting log, sit and, every once in a good while, get up and walk around.

In the winter, all the good logs are under the snow, so you have to sit in, well, the snow. And, you can't get up and walk around. You have to get up and snowshoe around. But, so what? Josh fires up his Gaz stove and we while away a few hours swapping lies while sipping cups of hot chocolate made more drinkable by ample doses of schnapps.

The views of Breckenridge, the Breckenridge Ski Area, and the Ten Mile Range were fairly easy on the eye. While we were hanging out, Josh laid some basic snow science stuff on us. Though we were told that the snow was very conducive to sliding right about then, he assured us that we were well away from anything even remotely resembling an avalanche area. This is like telling someone who is scared to death of snakes—while you're sitting in the jungle—that envenomation only occurs in about three-quarters of all snake bites. I spend the afternoon and evening perfectly convinced that, at any second, every snowflake on our side of Baldy, and quite possibly the vast majority of the snowflakes accumulated on the other side of Baldy, are going to slide their way directly into my schnapps and hot chocolate. There is nothing Josh can say to alleviate this concern, and he realizes it.

David joins us just before sunset. He arrives just in time for dinner, which consists of homemade barley, rice, and mushroom soup and French bread.

The sun is down by the time the chow is down, and it is getting cold fast. We're at about 11,000 feet and the early March winds are starting to blow chilly and cold. By 6:30, everyone is in their sleeping bags. All night, the wind howls. Our wind wall is not performing as well as we would have liked. Nonetheless, by 8 AM, Mark and I both feel like we should be awarded gold medals for Olympic marathon sleeping.

We now face a decision: we can fire up Josh's stove and eat in camp, or we can pack up and eat breakfast at the Blue Moose Restaurant in Breckenridge. We take the latter choice. By 9 AM, we're neck-deep in pancakes.

I sort of was thinking that we bailed out too quickly, that we should have hung out in camp a few hours longer, that it didn't really seem like a real camping trip. But the more I thought about it, the more I realized that we had just completed a very casual overnight trip in the backcountry. Maybe my personal ice has been broken with regards to winter camping, because "casual" was a description I would never have thought could be used to describe sleeping in the snow. And casual is the type of relationship I like most having with the backcountry.

Road Trip

My old amigo Curtis Robinson who, not coincidentally, was the very first editor of the paper I work for, has long espoused several road trip truths. And, since Curtis Robinson is, in my opinion, the all-time road trip champ of the cosmos, I have tended, over the years, to accept those truths not only as self-evident, but, concurrently, as gospel. It's not that Curtis Robinson is well traveled in the sense that he has visited Asia and Africa or anything. But, when it comes to pure numbers of miles spent in a moving vehicle, Curtis lives up where the snow leopards dwell.

I have known Curtis, who now lives in Aspen, to leave Kentucky, where he grew up, after work, with the goal of driving to Colorado to have a few beers with yours truly. Once here, he'd get up from the table less than an hour after arriving—as though he were preparing for a foray no more intense than visiting the men's room—saying words to the effect of, "Well, I'll be seeing ya'll later," as he strolled back to his car to drive back to Kentucky in time for work on Monday morning. And this has happened more times over the years than, as a random example, my wife, Gay, cares to remember.

As well, Curtis, for two years, essentially commuted from the northernmost reaches of California to work in the Los Angeles area—a distance of something like eight hundred miles. He didn't mind one bit, saying the drive home gave him the opportunity to unwind from work.

More than anyone I have ever met, Curtis Robinson loves to spend time in his car, or, for that matter, in anyone's car, as long as there's plenty of beer, several Tom Waits tapes, and enough vacant room in the backseat to hold several buckets of convenience store-procured fried chicken (a product that, in Curtis's learned opinion, contains every one of the four food groups: breasts, wings, thighs, and drumsticks).

The road trip-related truths Curtis has developed run something like this: the goal of any road trip worth its weight in stale barbecued potato chips ought not to be physical. It should be chronological and experiential. In other words, you shouldn't embark on a road trip to spend "x" amount of time in a place. You should embark on a road trip to be on the road, to be one with the road, and you should be not only ready and willing to accept any spontaneity that lies down in your path, but you should actively seek spontaneity out, if such a strategy is logically possible. I have known Curtis to leave on one of his infamous trips from Kentucky to Colorado, only to end up in Key West, which, on the surface, would seem like a tough thing to do, but if you know Curtis, it seems only natural. Also, Curtis believes that, unless you're averaging a thousand miles a day, you're not really taking a road trip, rather, you are "going for a drive."

I used to be a road trip aficionado myself, having driven cross-country many, many times without stopping, except for fuel, food, and more beer. But, as the years have worn on, I have tended to be less Curtis Robinson-like in my road trip habits. My wife and I usually do middle-aged things like stop for the night as we travel. And we don't drink beer every single second we're on the highway, an embarrassing admission that automatically makes us ineligible for the Curtis Robinson Road Trip Hall of Fame.

Now, you need to understand that my wife and I have spent a lot of time on the road. We've driven to Central America and back. We've driven to Mexico dozens of times. And we've traversed a large chunk of the Rockies. When we lived in Denver, we spent just about every single weekend on the road, because, not surprisingly, we simply had to get out of Denver as often as possible to maintain our sanity.

Since we have moved to the High Country though, our road trip mentality has waned. Because we already live in a great place, there's a lot less need to get out of Dodge at every damned opportunity. But, even when you dwell in the High Country, every once in a while you've got to hit the road, to lay your eyes on some different mountains, to drink in some different bars, to shoot the breeze with locals from other localities.

In the middle of the winter of 1994, both Gay and I found ourselves staring down the gullet of synchronized four-day weekends. Add that to the fact that those four days happened to fall on President's Day weekend—and I would rather poke myself in the eye with a shish kebob skewer than stay in Summit County during President's Day weekend because President's Day weekend is the busiest single three-day period hereabouts—and you have all the makings of a road trip mentality that could not possibly be stemmed by Hoover Dam on its best day.

We opted to head to Durango, a place Gay used to live, and a place that we've talked about maybe moving to when our time in Summit County is done. The plan was to spend one day driving down there, the next day skiing Purgatory, the next day being spontaneous, and then returning home on the fourth day. Now, I know such a weenie little road trip (850 miles, all told) would have Curtis Robinson rolling his eyes, wondering whatever happened to the M. John of old, but—what the hell?—sometimes you just take what you can get.

The first part of any road trip is making an initial getaway route determination. Since Gay and I generally head south whenever we have time enough to leave town (our vehicles won't even allow us to point them north), we always find ourselves flipping a coin: Leadville via Colorado 91 or Fairplay via Colorado 9. This time, Fairplay won out, so, we headed over 11,500-foot Hoosier Pass, full tank of gas in our 1991 Subaru Loyale station wagon, a couple of dozen tapes just burning to be played and, yes, a minuscule amount of tasty carbonated beverages.

We could not help but notice that storm clouds were building up in every direction as we left, a sure sign that the gods were paying attention to us, and that they had playfulness in their hearts. We did not consult a weather report before we left because, as we all know, weather reports in the High Country are about as accurate as snow depth reports issued by ski areas.

Gay and I have driven through Park County, which borders Summit County to the south, at least a billion times, because Gay's parents live in Cañon City, on the other side of Park County. Though the thought of living in Park County does not titillate me, I really like driving through it. I like the long views and the fact that, by and large, you can get away with driving at a high rate of speed thereabouts. Also, Park County is one of the best places in the state for wildlife viewing. Gay has seen a bear while driving through Park County, as well as several bald eagles. It's common to eyeball deer, elk, and antelope.

After descending from Trout Creek Pass into Chaffee County and the Arkansas River Valley, we detoured into Buena Vista for lunch. We stopped in some diner that we had never visited before and ate two of the greasiest burgers I have ever even heard of, much less consumed. Those burgers amounted to one of the few bad meals we've had in Buena Vista, and we have eaten many times in Buena Vista.

As its names indicates, Buena Vista (pronounced like a redneck from West Virginia would pronounce it, rather than how a Castilian would pronounce it), located at the base of the Collegiate Peaks, is one seriously beautiful place. It is a summer-only tourist town that caters major league to the Arkansas River's mammoth commercial rafting industry. It is a town that people traveling between Denver and Colorado Springs and the central Rockies stop in to eat, drink, and be merry. Thus, the restaurant scene is fairly evolved, which is certainly not the case in most of Colorado's small towns, where gourmet food is generally defined by whether or not the pickle on your burger is crispy or flaccid.

Gay and I have driven down the Arkansas River valley between Buena Vista and Poncha Pass enough times that both of our vehicles have every hill and curve memorized, allowing us to just put them on auto-pilot. And we love that drive. The Sawatch Range, being the highest in the state, is captivating, especially when storm clouds are moving over and between the peaks.

But, as lovely as the Sawatch Range is, we really dig the Sangre de Cristo Range, which is visible once you cross Poncha Pass into the expanse of the San Luis Valley. The "Valley," as it is known to friends, is one big bugger. Walled in on the east by the towering Sangres and on the west by the Cochetopa Hills, the Valley is a cattleperson's paradise, a veritable ocean of grass and down-home red-neckism. This is not the place to argue the validity of grazing on public land, lest you are game for a little fisticuffs.

The Valley is also home to the wonderfully weird Great Sand Dunes National Monument, which is visible from fifty miles away. The northern part of the San Luis Valley is one of the most sparsely populated areas of Colorado. The towns—Villa Grove, Hooper, Mosca, Saguache—are all dying little villages, almost depressing to behold. The buildings in those towns seem to be anchored to the ground so precariously that they could blow away at any moment, like the tumbleweeds that dominate the Valley's roadsides.

The one exception to this dying town observation is Crestone, which lies about fifteen miles off Colorado 17, just east of Moffat, at the base of the Sangres. Crestone is considered one of the spiritual meccas of the West (something to do with its being a card-carrying energy vortex or something) and, as such, has attracted just about every sort of worship-oriented person the world has to offer. There are colonies of Buddhists, Catholics, Druids, and New Agers, all living together in their own religion-specific facilities in this one off-the-beaten-path village, which happens to be located in one of the most scenic spots in the state.

I have only visited Crestone a few times and have always felt like some sort of anti-Fayhee harmonic convergence was about to converge directly on my head. I have never felt comfortable in Crestone and, judging from the very few conversations I have ever had there, Crestone doesn't exactly feel comfortable with me.

The one thing that does strike me as positive, or at least interesting, amidst all the sickeningly oppressive spirituality that dominates the Crestone landscape takes the form of sociological contrast. Colorado, more so than any other state I have ever lived in (and I have lived in nine), boasts an unbelievable amount of social differences between one town/county and another. This is not to say that the D.C. suburbs of northern Virginia do not differ drastically on many levels from the dying little coal towns of the Old Dominion's Appalachian Provinces. Nor is it to say that Santa Fe is not near-bouts a completely different world compared to Catron County, New Mexico.

It *is* to say that, at least when you are in Virginia—no matter where you are in Virginia—there are commonalities between parts of the state that are palpable. Ditto for New Mexico. No matter where you are in the Land of Enchantment, you know you are in the Land of Enchantment. But, in Colorado, you have conservative places like Crestone and, for that matter, the San Luis Valley, right down the road from the extreme hedonism and materialism of North America's preeminent ski counties. You have the desert lands of the Western Slope butting up against the High Country. You have the blighted neighborhoods of inner Denver a stone's throw from the Great Plains and even closer to mountain towns 9,000 feet above sea level. You have redneck (and damned proud of it), economically depressed Park County right across a pass from Breckenridge, one of the tackiest (and most affluent) tourist towns in the Rockies. And each of these places boasts its own variation of attitude.

It is almost disorienting. You walk all casual-like into a restaurant in Crestone and order a beer and a shot with lunch and you get looks from the waitpeople that you would expect to see in a dry county in the Deep South, whereas, just two hours before, you were sitting down to wet your whistle in the Manhattan Bar in Leadville, where the bartender looks at you funny if you don't order a shot with your beer.

As far as I am concerned, the San Luis Valley is where the American Southwest begins. And, as such, the place boasts a lot of fundamental sloppiness. Most of the homes have at least one junked car in the yard, along with several antique refrigerators, washers and dryers, and farm equipment of indeterminate lineage and function.

That's one of the things I like most about the Southwest. You don't have a large population of frenzied, nit-picking, whiny planners and code enforcement officials running around causing trouble all the damned time. And, if you did, that particular segment of the population would be threatened out of existence. How the whole planning and code enforcement professions came to think that junked cars in people's yards are unattractive visual features completely escapes me, as it does most people with a love of the great Southwest.

The cloud formations over the Sangres as we were driving through the Valley were some of the most stupendous we have ever seen. There can be no better place on earth for cloud viewing than a one-hundred-mile-long valley bordered by 14,000-foot-high peaks. We stopped in Saguache for liquid refreshments and to just stand there in the liquor store parking lot ogling at the clouds. Then we headed even further south, through increasing populations of bovines, beneath darkening skies, towards the town of Del Norte.

Del Norte used to be a much better place because there used to be a wonderful little Mexican restaurant right in the middle of town. But that restaurant closed several years ago and, as far as I am concerned, Del Norte now has no redeeming value whatsoever. Gay and I have been known to take five-hundred-mile detours for a good Mexican meal, and when a good Mexican restaurant closes its doors, we wear black armbands and lower our flag to half-mast.

I once almost ended up living in Del Norte. Just before I moved to Summit County to take a job at the *Summit Daily News*, I was offered a job editing the weekly papers in Del Norte, South Fork, and Creede, which are all owned by the same company. I almost took that job, because, first of all, they offered me a surprising amount of money and, secondly, I prefer working for weeklies more than dailies. Although, when you get right down to it, I really don't like working, period, especially for newspapers. But, Gay let me know in no uncertain terms that, if I thought she was going to move to Del Norte for any reason whatsoever, I had better think again.

As we drove through Del Norte on our way to Durango, I couldn't help but shudder at the thought of that town being the home turf of the Fayhees. As usual, Gay was right. Damn, I hate that about wives: they're always right.

The part of our road trip I was looking forward to most was crossing over Wolf Creek Pass, the snowiest pass in the state and one of the snowiest places in the nation. I had driven over Wolf Creek before, but that journey took place long ago, and it was in the summer, and we were going in the other direction.

With an average annual snowfall of almost five hundred inches, Wolf Creek is one of the most dangerous passes in Colorado when it comes to avalanches. When she lived in Durango, Gay found herself crossing Wolf Creek on numerous occasions in the worst weather conditions imaginable. As a result of several near-mishaps on Wolf Creek, my bride has developed a phobia about mountain passes in the winter, once again, indicating the depth and breadth of her intellect. She did not understand my enthusiasm for crossing this particular pass in a snowstorm but, then again, like most wives, there are parts of her husband's thought processes she will never understand, only tolerate. And that is the way it should be.

The mountains of southwestern Colorado are weird in that you can be in a completely snow-free valley one minute, then, two seconds later, you can find yourself driving through a scene that looks like it was transported straight from Baffin Island. It was snowing hard when we began ascending the pass and, by the time we reached the ski area near the summit, we were crawling along at 15 mph. I was happy as a pig in slop. I mean, if you're going to traverse one of the gnarliest passes in the country during the dead-on winter, you might as well do so in trying circumstances.

About a mile down the other side of the pass, it happened: off to the right, which, unfortunately, was the same side of the road we were on, what looked to be a fairly massive slide let loose faster than we could scream "SHITTTTT!" at two thousand decibels. I stopped the car, but the slide seemed to be headed straight towards us. We were both frozen with fear. We expected to be removed from the highway by a wall of snow posthaste. I held onto my beer with both hands, lest it slip out of my grip as we were being swept to our deaths by the avalanche that was getting closer and closer by the millisecond.

Then, we noticed some blinking lights in the bowels of the slide, which is not usual. It ended up being one of those kinds of snowplows that blow massive quantities of snow five hundred miles away as well as plowing it off the highway. What we had seen was not a slide at all but, rather, a heavy piece of machinery doing its job.

I pulled off the highway and ran back into the woods to clean out my underpants, and we went merrily on our way, tickled pink to not be dead.

Pagosa Springs is one of those towns that magazines like *Outside* contend is one of the up-and-coming, outdoor-kinda burgs in the Rockies. With a location midway between the Weminuche and South San Juan wilderness areas, such a contention is not all that hard to believe. But, man oh man, what an ugly little place. If it weren't for the fact that Meeker exists, Pagosa Springs would win my vote for the ugliest town in Colorado. And, even with that caveat, I believe Meeker and Pagosa tie for that dubious title. They ought to establish an Ugly Sister City relationship. Pagosa Springs, however, like most of southwestern Colorado, is experiencing some serious growth—but it is growth that is so tasteless it is beyond belief. I mean, Shreveport, Louisiana, is more quaint than Pagosa.

What we have in southwestern Colorado, to an extreme extent, is a tsunami of displaced Californians washing up on a shoreline of transplanted Texans. Unlike many of my fellow Coloradans, I happen to like both Texans and Californians, and I believe that ultimately, this state will benefit from the fact that, every year, several thousand people move here who have at least enough in the way of good sense to understand that Texas, despite its many charms, is just too damned hot and that California, despite its amazing beauty, is just too damned fucked up.

But (and there is no way to say this tactfully), both Texans and Californians bring with them a lot of superiority complex baggage. They each, basically, think their own shit don't stink and, while that may prove to be unnerving for a lot of Coloradans who already live in the areas that are being inundated by Californians and Texans, it at least makes for some amusing cultural spectating. Whenever one has the opportunity to observe the irresistible force of Chablis and pasta salad going head-to-head with the immovable object of Lone Star beer and barbecue, one ought to just pull up a lawn chair and watch.

By the time we reached Durango, six-and-a-half hours after leaving Summit County, it was obvious that we were in for some funky weather. As it turned out, in three days, Purgatory Ski Area received almost three feet of fresh snow.

I had only been to Durango twice before. The first time was for about an hour on our way back to Denver (the long way, which is generally the best way) from the Telluride Bluegrass Festival in 1986. Gay and I stopped only long enough to buy our wedding rings, which means that Durango holds a near and dear place in our hearts because, even though our marriage, like most marriages, has its ups and downs, through thick and thin, we both still really like those rings. Then, two summers ago, after I finished hiking the Colorado Trail, I spent one night in Durango.

Durango is sort of like an outdoor enthusiast's definition of Mecca in Colorado. It is a town that just about everyone I know would like to move to, except that it is so economically unpredictable and so far removed from the Colorado mainstream, it doesn't even seem like a real place sometimes. I know a lot of people who have lived a long time in Colorado who have never visited Durango. It is justifiably perceived by High Country dwellers as being part of our fifty-first state: Four Corners.

We got a room in an EconoLodge, where prices for a room this time of year are literally half of what they are in the summer. Then we hit downtown. Durango, like Summit County, has a brew pub, which we visited very soon after arriving. Most brew pubs in Colorado are, when you get right down to it, not that great. They draw customers because visiting brew pubs is a popular thing to do these days, rather than because brew pub beer is anything special. But Durango Beer is almost as good as Breckenridge Brew Pub beer, and that's a mighty big compliment.

We ate dinner at an organic Chinese restaurant, and the meal was great. The service, however, was spotty, which is something we noticed all over southwestern Colorado. Unlike Summit County, there is a fairly substantial New Mexico-esque, hippy-dippy, Grateful Dead influence in southwestern Colorado. And, as much as I am a big fan of attitudinal and sociological diversity, the aforesaid stereotype does not translate well to the service industries.

At the Chinese restaurant, our waitress spaced out our soup, which ended up being okay, because the entrees were huge. Now, it's not like this was the first time I've had soup spaced out by a waitperson. But, usually, somewhere along the line, it dawns on the waitperson that they screwed up, and they come running over, red-faced and apologetic, offering to comp you whatever it was they forgot. Not this lady. She just mellowed her way through the evening, oblivious to her incompetence. It was actually kind of funny.

The next morning, after eating far too much breakfast at Carver's, we drove to Purgatory. I was actually kind of surprised. I had expected it to be a smaller version of a hyper-modern Summit County ski area. Rather, it ended up being a mom and pop kind of place, with antique lifts and a high percentage of skiers wearing not exactly the latest in alpine fashions. We fit right in.

It was also extremely crowded. I have never waited in lift lines that long or slow-moving. (Seems President's Day is also celebrated in the San Juans.) Gay, who grew up skiing Monarch and Crested Butte, said it reminded her of how things used to be in Colorado, back before the days of high-speed quads and such. When it comes to skiing, one clearly gets spoiled in a place like Summit County.

This marked the first time I had ever really skied powder. And, on those rare occasions when I was actually skiing, rather than waiting in line, I found powder to be as cool as everyone in the High Country always says it is. Of course, having never really skied powder, I never really learned how to ski powder. Thus, before the morning was over, I found myself experiencing my very first alpine face plant. And, you know what? There is a reason why face plants are so named. You really do plant your face, the same way you would plant a shrubbery. I had snow up my nose, under my eyelids, and between my teeth. Interesting experiencew.

Before leaving Durango the next morning, we stopped in the Toh-Atin Gallery, the place where we bought our wedding bands, seemingly one hundred years ago. As far as I am concerned, Toh-Atin is by far the best Southwest/Native American gallery in Colorado. Having lived in New Mexico for five years, I generally have a bad taste in my mouth when it comes to southwestern art. I consider the vast majority of it to be pure schlock. But, Toh-Atin is amazing. I could easily spend every cent I own there, and I wouldn't even scratch the surface of my avarice. Of course, I could spend every cent I own there and not actually have enough money to buy anything, because we're talking some expensive stuff here.

Our plan for the day was to hang out in Mesa Verde National Park, a place I had not visited in fifteen years. We drove a little ways in, but turned around because it was snowing to beat the band. We promised ourselves to return there in the spring.

This is a weird part of the state, and Mesa Verde drives that weirdness home like no other place. Colorado is probably the most culturally sterile state in the West, and the backbone of that cultural sterility stems, at least in part, from our relative lack of Native Americans. We have only two reservations, Ute Mountain and Southern Ute, both of which are south of Mesa Verde, on the New Mexico border. And that's it. In a state that was once dominated by Utes, Kiowas, Arapahoes et al., all we have left are of that heritage are place names and those two relatively small reservations. When I lived in New Mexico, I attempted to interact with the ample Native American culture there as much as my blue-eyed self could. And I considered that interaction to be one of the most wonderful aspects of my five years in the Land of Enchantment. Up where I live, in the High Country, the only interaction we have with pre-white man times takes the form of ghosts and legends.

We ate at McDonalds in Cortez, then pointed the car towards Telluride.

The highway from Cortez, over Lizard Head Pass, to Telluride, is one of the few paved mountain roads in Colorado I had not driven. Neither had Gay. Again, I was really looking forward to it, while Gay was wondering what on earth was possessing us to be driving over yet another pass in a dead-of-winter snowstorm.

We stopped for gas in Dolores, which ended up being a sweet little town, although it appeared to be dominated by businesses catering to fisherpeople and hunters. Not my kind of place. Then, forty miles later, we passed through Rico, a town I have long longed to visit. I met a couple from Rico on the Colorado Trail, and they told me it was an old mining ghost town that was coming back to life because Telluride employees who could no longer afford to live in Telluride were moving there. (Sort of the Alma or Minturn of Telluride.) I was surprised that Rico was a bonafide high-altitude town, with an elevation of almost 9,000 feet. It was also the kind of place that demanded you get out of your car and walk around for a bit. There were old, dilapidated buildings interspersed with remodeled Victorian homes and log cabins. There was a very enticing saloon. But, since it was still snowing hard, and, since we still had to drive over the pass, we moved on without so much as wetting our whistles.

For some reason, I had thought that Lizard Head was one of the state's worst passes. But, it ended up being pretty easy. So, by 2 PM, we found ourselves mirthfully parked in a bar in Telluride, enjoying a few pints of Fat Tire ale, which is brewed in Fort Collins.

Telluride is a town that is going to hell in a handbasket, development-wise, so fast it's unbelievable. It is the only ski town in the state that I believe rivals Breckenridge when it comes to senseless, ugly, fast-paced overdevelopment. Once again, the Californians are bumping up against the Texans, and the result is predictable. Telluride sucks on all levels, except for the awesome beauty of the surrounding mountains.

We drove on to Ouray, where we decided to spend the night. As it was Gay's fortieth birthday the next day, we got a nice room in the Hotel St. Elmo, a bed and breakfast so cute and quaint it automatically puts even a schmuck like me in a romantic mood. Of course, it was also fairly pricey, so we had to eat dinner in a diner rather than in someplace decent, like the Hotel St. Elmo's highly regarded restaurant.

For reasons that still escape us, we both ordered chicken fried steak at a local greasy spoon, and it was the worst meal we had eaten in several decades. The meat was clearly not from a cow, the mashed potatoes were stolen from the local elementary school cafeteria, and the gravy was made from a drywall compound.

After such a hideous meal, we headed on over to the only open bar in town (Ouray doesn't exactly rock in the winter), where we were the only patrons. We shot a game of pool, and called it a night, having pretty much done Ouray. (I should note that Ouray, known as the Switzerland of Colorado, is justifiably a very busy place in the summer.)

It was still snowing like mad. On our way back to the hotel, a small car, coming down from Silverton and Red Mountain Pass, managed to navigate its way under the wheels of a tractor-trailer going the opposite direction. The car was trashed, but no one was hurt. It was clearly the most exciting event that had transpired in Ouray for many a moon. Back at the hotel, we played a little Trivial Pursuit, watched a little tube, and hit the sack.

By morning, the Subaru had eighteen inches of snow on it. The town was buried. As we made our way down Main Street towards Montrose, Ouray, which is my second-favorite town in Colorado, after Crested Butte, had the look of a place that has been buried by snowstorms so many times that the townspeople don't even think about it any more.

It boggles my mind that Ouray is not the absolute physical embodiment of a small, isolated, winter-dominated town in Colorado. About thirty miles further south, there's Silverton, the most remote town in the state, a place that gets snowed in for a week or two nearbouts every winter. We had talked about driving from Durango straight to Ouray via Colorado 550, but Gay rightly pointed out that, with all the snow the San Juans were receiving, there was a good chance that we would have to spend the rest of the winter in Silverton if we chose that route. And, as much as I like Silverton, the thought of being snowed in there for more than about twenty minutes does not appeal to me.

To the east, the storm clouds were still looking mean and nasty, so we decided to take the long way home, through Grand Junction, which is not exactly a cop-out, because the views of Colorado National Monument, the Grand Mesa, and the Book Cliffs along that route are tremendous. I really like this part of the state, and maybe one day we will move over here, where it's generally warm and sunny. But, after we got back to Summit County, I looked around at this place, the place I live, and realized for not exactly the first time that, as much cool stuff as there is in Colorado, the Summit ranks right up there. This place, in and of itself, makes for a wonderful road trip destination.

Even Curtis Robinson would have to agree with that.

Clinging to the Psychic Belay

I'm not certain, psychologically, at what point enlightened concern about a potentially sphincter-puckering situation crosses over into the realm of overt fear (and vice-versa), and, from there, into the realm of a bonafide phobia. When it comes to rock climbing, or, more accurately, when it comes to *me* rock climbing, the question has to be asked in exactly that context. Am I afraid of heights? (Overt fear.) Or am I afraid of falling? (Enlightened concern.) Or, am I afraid of even thinking about heights and falling? (Phobia.)

There is a distinction here, and, for reasons that probably have more to do with an impending midlife crisis than they do with anything resembling good sense, I decided one spring to seek an answer to those questions. So, I signed up for the beginners rock climbing class offered by the Breckenridge Campus of Colorado Mountain College and taught by Keith Robine.

It's not that this is completely virgin territory. I've climbed more than a few times before. I was actually born fairly dexterous and coordinated and balanced in the climbing realm. I once took a one-day climbing class in Estes Park and performed not as badly as some of the other students. And I have visited indoor climbing walls a dozen or so times, managing on more than one occasion to make it to the top of some marked routes without overtly "cheating" every step of the way.

Still, I had been thinking for a year or two that it would be good to actually get to the point where I could go out to some remote climbing site, with a buddy or two and a twenty-foot-high pile of gear, and actually climb—outside without an instructor. Just me, my amigos, and those nagging questions about fear and phobia dancing their little dance in the deepest recesses of my psyche.

The older I get, the more I have come to understand how important it is to participate in activities that cause a little nervous sweat to form on the brow. This is not to say that I plan on taking up shark wrestling any time soon. It is to say that purposely seeking fear out and establishing a rapport with it is not necessarily a bad thing. It may not keep you young, but it may help keep you from getting old.

Robine has been climbing for most of his adult life and teaching climbing almost as long. I don't really know how he rates as a climber, because I have not yet developed a learned enough eye to make that judgment, but that's less important than how well he teaches climbing. After learning to climb the way most people learn to climb, from other climbers out on the rock (in this case, in New England), Robine decided to institutionalize the teaching part of his climbing expertise through an eight-month extensive and intensive program offered by Denver-based Outdoor Leadership Training Seminars (OLTS), one of the most respected of these kinds of programs in the world.

After finishing his course of study (it should be noted that Robine also carries a math degree from MIT and taught math for several years), it was off to Thailand, where he organized the operations in that country for world-renowned SOBEK, a California-based adventure travel company that has since merged with Mountain Travel.

With this potpourri of experience under his belt, Robine moved to Breckenridge, where, for several years, he taught many different classes for Colorado Mountain College, including climbing, math, geography, Tai Chi, orienteering, cross-country skiing, and outdoor leadership skills. This is a man well versed in how to set up and operate a beginners' climbing class. He could probably do it in his sleep, which is good.

We get together for the first time on a Wednesday evening, in a classroom, for an hour. The purpose of this gathering is fundamental orientation and to get to know each other a little bit. Or, failing that, at least to learn each other's names.

Robine puts us through a drill that is designed to build teamwork. We all get in a circle, and randomly grab each other's hands. You can't grab the hand of either of the people next to you, and you can't grab both hands of the same person. The result is a tangled mess of criss-crossed arms.

Once this is accomplished, the group tries to untangle itself. This is about the fifth time I've participated in this exercise over the years, and I have never liked it, at least partially because, among the many levels my mind does not work, problem solving of this type is one of them. If IQ is measured even partially by one's ability to sort out these kinds of physical problems, then I am objectively even stupider than I am subjectively.

Anyhow, as a group, after about thirty minutes of trying, we fail to untangle the knot. This may or may not have implications and deep meaning. If it does, Robine is keeping it to himself.

We talk for a while about our upcoming class schedule. We will spend one Saturday morning together in the Breckenridge Recreation Center, learning the most basic of climbing basics. If the weather is nice, or at least not too bad, in the afternoon we will head towards Ten Mile Canyon, where we will actually climb on real rock. If the weather is bad, we will stay in the rec center and climb on the highly rated indoor climbing wall there.

Then, two weekends after that, we will meet and drive down to the Platte River Valley, near Pine, and spend two full days climbing on some of the better known, and most beautiful rock in the state. Robine also tells us we each need to procure a harness, a locking carabiner, a figure-eight, and, if possible, climbing shoes. With only three days before we meet again, this need to score gear comes as something of a surprise to the class. Nevertheless, everyone there gathered, all twelve students, shows up the following Saturday armed and ready for more than a little climbing action.

I hesitate, climbing sub-novice that I am, even after having finished the class I'm telling you about here, to even pretend that I know enough about this wonderful sport to make sport-specific observations. It's one thing to paint verbal impressions, quite another to say, "This is the way it is," regarding any component of climbing. The one exception to my trepidation here is this: climbing, in all its manifestations, incarnation, and variations, is Serious Bidness. You can be jovial of spirit and demeanor, joking around and all, but, when the nut is cut, you need to have the ability to not only fake being tightly wrapped while involved in any and all parts of the climbing experience, but you need to actually *be* tightly wrapped, lest someone makes the journey to meet Buddha as a result of your lack of tightly wrappedness.

This reality, not surprisingly, formed the backbone of Robine's instructional process. He introduced us in patient, some would say repetitive, detail to the language of climbing—what you say and when you say it, so there is no miscommunication whatsoever (because even the slightest miscommunication while climbing can have dire consequences)—and to the art of rope handling.

For the most part, especially at our level, one does not use the rope for climbing, unless one is not climbing so well and, therefore, needs a little help to progress one inch further. Rather, one uses the rope to catch one's carcass if one falls. The rope does not do this itself. Neither do you. You need a partner. One of you is the climber, the other of you is the belayer. By far, the belayer is the more important of the two, for it is he/she who makes it so the rope catches you if and when you fall victim to gravity.

For most beginner classes, "top-roping" is used. This is where the rope is attached, by whatever means or combination of means, to something at the top of the section of rock you want to climb. At the rec center, this means wrapping the rope around a metal bar at the top of the climbing wall that exists solely for this purpose. Out on the rock, it means hiking up and around to the top of whatever it is you plan to climb and utilizing whatever means to safely secure the rope. (You can attach the rope to trees, rocks, or both.) Then you hike back down to the bottom of the rock and begin your climbing procedures.

When you get more advanced, you actually place protection, which will then arrest your butt if you fall, as you climb. This takes a lot of experience and a lot of climbing hardware. It will be some time before a raw beginner such as myself is ready to place protection.

These aforesaid procedures are not deceptively simple; they actually are simple. The climber basically ties him/herself into their harness with one end of the rope, while the belayer basically does the same with the other end, using their figure-eight and their locking carabiner. You take a moment to check each other out, making certain everything has been done correctly. There is no ego here; it's perfectly socially acceptable to examine the rope work of the person in whose hands your life rests. As the climber climbs, the belayer takes up the slack in the rope. If the climber falls, the belayer yanks back on the rope, disallowing any rope slippage, and the fall is almost instantly arrested. When the climber reaches the top, or a point in the climb where he can proceed no further, the belayer lets slack out of the rope and lowers the climber down.

It really is that straight forward, which, in a way, is bad. After all, if this were rocket science, you could be forgiven for screwing up and letting your partner fall thirty feet to his/her death. With this simplicity thing, you're pretty much left excuseless if you screw up and medical trauma results.

We end up practicing all this stuff all day at the rec center, because the weather is too bad to venture out to Ten Mile Canyon. Even though hardly anyone else in the class has even pretended to climb before, everyone does well. And everyone seems genuinely into it. Robine seems somewhat relieved.

After Robine makes a few generic observations about individuals and the group, we are dismissed. We are to meet in two weeks, for a journey into the real world of climbing.

The Platte Canyon is one of Colorado's most spectacular, though lesser-known, paradises. Part of the Pike's Peak Uplift, this region boasts hundreds of square miles of the most amazing rock formations in the state. We drive to Sphinx Rock, about a mile from beautiful downtown Pine, and about half a mile from one of the coolest bars in the Rockies, the Buck Snort.

It takes us (and by "us," I mean, "Robine, with the rest of the class standing there watching") over an hour to fix three routes up the side of Sphinx Rock. Each of these routes has its very own rope, which is attached so solidly to the top that you could tie the two ends dangling far down below to the bumper of a semi-truck that immediately cruised off at 100 mph, and all that would happen would be that you'd have to untie the bumper sooner or later. Robine uses a dizzying and dazzling array of climbing hardware, the use of which will escape us, except in the most general sense, for some time to come, to attach the ropes. He has already eye-balled three climbing "lines" (which look no different than the rest of the rock to the rest of us), and each of the ropes hangs reassuringly plus-or-minus along those lines. After one more safety lecture, Robine sets us loose, under the close scrutiny of the two assistant instructors, Nola and Bobby, whose last names I don't know.

I was one of the first to climb, though it should be noted that I purposefully chose the easiest-looking of those lines. A lady named Sheila was my belayer. Once the climber and the belayer are tied in to the rope, this is the conversation that transpires before any climbing can take place:

Climber: "On belay?" (Meaning: "You got my butt covered, Jackson?")

Belayer: "Belay on." (Meaning: "I gotcha covered, Holmes.")

Climber: "Climbing." (Meaning: "Pay serious attention, starting *now!*")

Belayer: "Climb on." (Meaning: "Climb on.")

Sheila and I went through all this, as per protocol and as per good sense and, suddenly, I was faced with this, like, seventy-foot-high slab of rock that was very much unlike, in all ways I could think of on the spot, the climbing wall at the rec center. First of all, unlike the rec center wall, there are no pretty little pieces of colored tape showing you what holds to use if you desire to follow a "pure" route. Second, there are no pretty little pieces of colored tape showing you what holds to use. And, third, there are no pretty little pieces of tape . . . You have to eye-ball the rock face for hand and foot holds all by yourself.

Also, and this was pretty noticeable and attention-riveting, there were no holds to speak of at all. What an interesting development. There were plenty of microscopic nubs of rock protrusions occurring about every fourteen feet, but, that was it. This, combined with the fact that none of the students had climbing shoes, made our initial attempts at ascents "deliberate" in their pace. I was wearing old running shoes that, on the rock, might as well have had Crisco smeared on their soles. For every inch I gained vertically, my feet ran the equivalent of the Boston Marathon at a sprinter's pace.

Two hundred years later, I made it to the top, so damned tired I couldn't have mustered the energy to move my arms if a Tasmanian devil walked up and started gnawing on my elbow. I still, however, had to descend, and this is where you put your trust in a very captivating combination of (1) technology that you have not yet learned to trust, and (2) a person, your belayer, who, for all you know, might hate your guts for some reason you are not even aware of. What you do is lean back, at about a ninety-degree angle, to the rock, and "walk" your way down, with the belayer letting out the necessary amount of slack as you descend.

This is assuredly the point where one's psyche starts examining the nature of, and the relationships between, enlightened concern, overt fear, and a bonafide phobia. I have always felt fairly uncomfortable with heights, which is unarguably the natural state of all human beings. Though you can condition yourself to deal with heights, as real climbers demonstrate every day, and your immediate relationship to heights, instinctively, your mind, at moments like when you're fifty feet up in the air "standing" at a ninety-degree angle to a huge ol' slab of rock, goes on red alert. Internally, there are bells and sirens and whistles and red lights going off, and your internal information-relaying system is trying to convince your motor operations center to get in gear and start remedying what clearly is an undesirable set of circumstances *at your earliest* goddamned convenience.

At this point, controlled breathing is a good thing, because your mind may start to wander around like a man dying of thirst in the middle of the Sonoran Desert in June. You may start thinking about physics, about how that rope, upon which you are relying heavily at this moment, is nothing more than a series of teensy little molecules that are bound together by something known to the scientific world as "unexplainable magic." Yet, at the same time, there's also this gravity thing that, though equally unexplainable, at least has the benefit of familiarity. We all *know* what gravity does. We, as beginner-level climbers, do not yet know what climbing ropes do, or, of more concern, what they maybe don't do.

When I got down, everyone applauded and said what a good job I did. I went over and sat down in the shade for a few minutes, performing a cranial scan. Did this undertaking make any sense on any level? Did I want to rest up and tackle another climb, knowing full well that the next step would be even harder, the consequences of a mistake even more devastating? Well, of course I didn't. I wanted to pack my things up and drive to the Buck Snort and drink myself into a stupor. That, after all, is the wise choice, an action easily justified, easily understood.

But, alas, that's not the choice I made. As I sat there watching my classmates, most of whom were actually pretty good at this climbing thing—much better than I—struggling up Sphinx Rock, giggling at their successes and grimacing at their exertions and scratching their heads over their failures, I said what the hell? The only thing to fear is the lack of fear itself. As long as I was scared doo-doo-less, I would likely do all right. And, anyway, the only way to learn what I wanted to learn about fear was to be fearful.

It was time to visit with the rock once again, to work on the psychic belay.

Janet's Cabin

To be honest, the thought of spending a night at Janet's Cabin—or, for that matter, any backcountry hut or cabin—has never captivated me. I know people who are cabin junkies, people who would rather hike, ski, or snowshoe to a cabin than participate in any other form of outdoor recreation, including, but not limited to, orgies.

I am not one of them. I have spent a fair number of nights in backcountry cabins and huts (mostly along the Appalachian Trail in New Hampshire), covering the gamut from thoroughly rustic to downright civilized, and I cannot remember having what I could truly characterize as a pleasant time at any of those facilities. I mean, I have met some fun people while staying in backcountry huts, and I have even participated in a few wild and wacky hut-centered parties. But, when it's time to venture to the "land of nod," if you're staying in a hut or cabin, you oftentimes wind up in a room full of snoring, flatulent, tossing-and-turning people named Louie from the Bronx who, while being perfectly acceptable Trivial Pursuit opponents around the communal dining table at 7 PM, are not the sorts of hombres you really want to find yourself sleeping one foot from in a poorly ventilated dormitory room.

When you stay the night in a cabin or hut, you place yourself at the mercy of the fates. You could end up with a cabin full of Swedish

Bikini Team members who are hell bent for a night of serious hedonism. Or, you could end up with the board of directors of the loyal order of geeks, social misfits, and those who deplore spending time on personal hygiene. The latter scenario, or something very much akin to it, I should point out, seems to happen a little more often than the Swedish Bikini Team thing, which, I'm certain, surprises the heck out of everyone.

Any time I have had the motive, opportunity, and means of getting my carcass out into the woods for any period longer than a couple of hours, I would much rather camp away from the maddening hut-and-cabin-seeking masses. Which is fine, except for the fact that I am not what you would call an enthusiastic winter camper. It's not that I mind the cold as much as I mind having to retire to the tent at 5 PM. I count sleeping as one of my favorite activities in the world, but even I have my limits on the number of hours I can comfortably stay in the sack and, during winter camping, that number of hours is generally exceeded by a factor of two. Also, getting up to visit the little boys' room in the middle of the night while winter camping is not the most rapturous experience in the world.

Problem is, toward the end of the long High Country winter, I really start missing multi-day backcountry trips. I get antsy to sleep under the stars. And March is the time of year when that antsiness really starts becoming a major distraction in my life. So, when photographer Mark Fox asked me one March if I would be interested in joining him for a one-night foray to Janet's Cabin, I overcame my natural reluctance to venture anywhere near backcountry huts and answered with an enthusiastic affirmative.

We called up Leigh Girvin Yule, secretary of Summit Huts Association, and she set us up with a minimum of fuss. We asked a friend, Mike Kurth, to come along. So, one Thursday in the height of ski season, along about the crack of noon, we started making our way towards one of Summit County's most popular winter attractions.

I don't remember who decided we would snowshoe up instead of ski. I am a pretty poor skier, and my backcountry skiing experience has always been limited to day-long, light-touring trips. I have never skied with a full pack on my back, and I knew full well that, if I tried,

I would likely spend the entire trip tweezering tree bark out of my facial skin. I agreed with the snowshoe plan.

Mark had a pair of Tubbs aluminum snowshoes. Snowshoeing is going through what has to be considered Boom Times these days, and I have seriously considered buying myself a pair. This trip would help me make that decision. I rented a pair just like Mark's, which are medium-sized, because Mark spends a lot of time tromping through hip-deep snow looking for good camera angles, as well as private places to relieve himself and, thus, needs the high degree of floatation afforded by larger shoes. Mike rented a smaller pair, because he assumed before the fact that, as popular as Janet's Cabin is, the trail up to it would likely be very packed. Mike assumed absolutely correctly. The small shoes were perfect, and Mike ended up being able to walk a lot faster as a result.

In order to spend the night at Janet's Cabin, you have to rent a space. Summit Huts sends you all sorts of printed material, like liability waivers and a parking pass for Copper Mountain. You park at Copper, near the transportation building in the area reserved for Janet's Cabin patrons. Then, you take the shuttle to Union Creek, where you hand over your trail voucher.

You are then issued a lift ticket. Yes, I am almost embarrassed to admit it, but a backcountry foray to Janet's Cabin (located up Guller Creek along the Colorado Trail, just below Searle Pass, at 11,618 feet) begins with some bold-faced cheating on the access front. You take the K and L lifts up, cutting probably a thousand feet off your ascent.

You get a fair number of strange looks when getting on and off a lift while carry snowshoes and a full backpack. Butt-tuckers look at you funny, as do skiers. So you kill them on the spot. Actually, you don't have to ride the lift up. Were you so disposed, you could simply snowshoe or ski your way up to the trailhead, which is located about a half-mile down Copper Mountain's West Tenmile ski run. We opted to go ahead and take the lift, at least partially because Mark and I had exercised some recreational indiscretion the night before, and we were not feeling fit as fiddles.

The weather was more perfect than perfect, the kind of day that makes one erroneously start thinking that spring has sprung. It was the kind of day that makes you start shedding. It was the kind of day where it would have been nice if I had remembered to bring my baseball hat. Even with sunblock, my face started feeling scorched within about fifteen seconds of disembarking—in a most uncoordinated fashion, I might add—from the lift.

From the trailhead, it's about a half-mile of downhill before you reach Guller Creek. We snowshoed for only a few minutes before we caught up with our first group of Janet's Cabin-bound compadres—two couples from Denver, sporting rented telemark gear. One of the women was not, uh, such a good skier. We came across her as she was trying to stand up after having crashed and burned in a fairly impressive fashion. I thanked what limited intellect I boast for steering my internal decision-making process towards snowshoes rather than skis, because, if I had tried to ski down that first hill with a full pack on, I would surely have died. Not only was it steep, but the snow was very hard packed and icy. In addition, most of the descent boasted multiple fall lines, which I consider the terrain feature from hell when it comes to skiing.

The descent was difficult enough that I slipped several times on the snowshoes, even though I, like Mike and Mark, was using cross-country ski poles to help me keep my balance. Snowshoe technology has increased so much in the past few years that the sport itself has been revolutionized. Not only have the shoes themselves undergone significant design changes, but the binding systems have metamorphosed to the degree that they have little or nothing in common with the bindings of yesteryear, except for the fact that they are designed to attach boot-adorned human feet to snowshoes.

One of the things that makes modern-day bindings so effective is that they boast a pivoting claw on the bottom. As you ascend or descend, this claw digs into terra firma—well, actually, terra snowa—in such a way that, if you have any balance whatsoever, your chances of slipping are almost nil. Side-to-side, however, is a horse of a different color. And, with packed snow and multiple fall-lines, that different-colored equine reared its mischievous head directly in my Here & Now numerous times. Though I never went head over heels or anything, I almost did just that several times—something that would have amused my camera-toting associate mightily.

You gain more than one thousand feet from the top of the L Lift to Janet's Cabin, spread out over the course of maybe four or five miles.

By Colorado standards, that has to be considered about as mellow as a backcountry trip gets. And, though I have mentioned how we were carrying full packs, we weren't carrying packs that were, well, full.

Because we were staying in a cabin, there was no need for a tent. Since that cabin boasts a wood-burning stove and gas heat, we did not need to carry heavy sleeping bags. And since the cabin has propane cooking facilities (the propane bottles being carried up by helicopter), we did not have to carry cook-kits, fuel bottles, or stoves.

At the same time, Summit Huts Association justifiably tries to put the equipment-based fear of God into people planning to visit Janet's Cabin. In addition to stressing numerous times in its literature that one has to have one's ducks in a huddle vis-à-vis backcountry travel in the winter, Summit Huts asks that people going to Janet's Cabin carry enough in the way of survival gear and extra clothing to outfit an ambitious Everest expedition. There is no doubt those recommendations are wise. After all, any time you start approaching tree line in Colorado in the winter, you're asking for serious weather.

I ended up carrying just about every single item on the Summit Huts equipment list. The entire time I was packing, I was thinking how humiliating it would be to get lost in a white-out and have search and rescue come in looking for us with all the Denver TV stations doing live satellite feeds on the progress of the search, while all our buddies were down at the Moose Jaw drinking beer and taking bets on whether or not we would make it out in one piece. So, I carried enough in the way of clothing that, if I put even half of it on, I would have to walk like a cross between the Michelin Man and the Pillsbury Doughboy.

By the time we stopped for lunch, we were all soaked through with sweat. I cannot remember such a warm and sunny day this time of year. It was amazing.

On the way up, we passed several parties that had spent the previous night at the cabin. The first consisted of four backcountry snowboarders. These guys had snowshoed up, spent the day before boarding on and around Searle Pass, then boarded down.

I am really happy to see that snowboarding is starting to become more and more popular in the backcountry, although, I must admit I have no earthly idea whether the snowboarders in the backcountry are ex-backcountry skiers, or whether they are snowboarders who are venturing away from ski areas. And that kind of makes a difference in the context of my next point.

I have long felt the current warlike mentality that exists between skiers and boarders is something not likely to last for many more years. The two camps simply have too many obvious mutual interests to remain enemies. And, being a backcountry enthusiast, I look at the backcountry as the best venue for people of disparate views and interests coming, if not to agreement, then at least to some semblance of understanding.

We also passed two couples skiing down from Janet's Cabin pulling sleds with young children. Holy stinky diapers, Batman, the notion that I might be sharing Janet's Cabin with sub-adults had not entered my head. It's not that I think children should be banned from Janet's Cabin, or anything, it's just that I would, if given a choice, rather none be there at the same time as, you know, me.

It took us about three hours to make it to the cabin, by which time we were all remarkably fatigued. Even with the newer, more-streamlined and lighter snowshoes, you still have to walk differently enough when snowshoeing that you utilize either different muscles than when you normally walk, or you use the same muscles more intensely. Whatever the cause, my legs were really spent by the time we got there at 3 PM, and my legs usually do not get tired after only three hours on the trail with a lighter-than-normal pack on my back.

Janet's Cabin is truly a remarkable facility. I once visited it a few months before it was officially opened in the winter of 1988, and I remember being awestruck then by the design, the craftsmanship, and the technology. After spending one night there, I have not lost that feeling. I would admire Janet's Cabin if it was located on a cul-de-sac in Denver.

Named in memory of Janet Boyd Tyler, an avid skier who succumbed to cancer in 1988, Janet's Cabin cost more than $300,000 to build. It is the first of a planned five- to seven-cabin Summit Huts system that, when completed, will connect Copper Mountain, Frisco, Breckenridge, Keystone, and Montezuma. (The next Summit Huts facility, Francie's Cabin, located near Breckenridge, is scheduled to be completed by fall 1994.)

Janet's Cabin boasts three propane cooking stoves, a propane heating stove, photo-voltaic-powered electric lights, state-of-the-art indoor composting toilets, two sinks, a fully equipped kitchen, beds with mattresses and pillows, a hutmaster's quarters (which is where we were housed), and—get this—a sauna. We're not exactly talking about roughing it here.

We settled our gear in the downstairs hutmaster's quarters, which has its own kitchen facilities and bedroom, and headed straight out onto the sun-drenched deck. This is one seriously wonderful deck, a great place to enjoy a schnapps-laced beverage or two hundred. The view is straight up to Searle Pass, over which the Colorado Trail passes.

While people like Mark, Mike, and I look at a trip to and from Janet's Cabin as just that—a trip to and from Janet's Cabin—most people look at it as a base of operations for backcountry, ski-oriented day trips. They headquarter themselves at Janet's Cabin, but spend most of the day out skiing in the boonies.

One group that was already there when we arrived, however, was spending their day not out skiing, but, rather, digging a snow cave. These three guys ended up being a little on the strange side. We never did figure out why the hell they were digging a snow cave, but, when they spotted our schnapps and rum supply, which, I'll admit, was reasonably substantial, they commented on the fact that perhaps we were a little over-stocked on the refreshment front. It wasn't exactly like we were drunkenly running around naked while reciting bawdy limericks, or anything. We were just sitting there, enjoying the ambiance of Janet's Cabin with beverages in hand. So, we decided that, if any unseemly schnapps-related behavior did come from the three of us, we would be certain to direct it towards that particular trio.

Not long after we arrived, the foursome with the bad skier pulled in. Shortly after that, two of their friends arrived. (This six-tet hailed from Denver.) Later, a group of four gnarly, backcountry-skiing-crazed Montanans arrived. All told, we were joined by twenty people that night, which is about seventeen or eighteen more people than I usually hang out with in the backcountry.

Every person there, besides us, had spent numerous nights in huts. They were obviously very comfortable with the whole hut set-up. We felt a little out-of-place and, therefore, uncomfortable, so, shortly after dark, we went downstairs into the hutmaster's quarters to cook and eat dinner. Since we didn't have to worry about carrying cooking gear, we had opted to splurge a little on our chow. We had hot and sour soup, salami, cheese and crackers, a roasted chicken, and pasta.

And, for dessert, we had that all-American post-dinner favorite: candy bars and more schnapps, washed down with a touch of Jagermeister (to aid the digestion, you understand).

Mark went out in the frigid night to take photos (man, once again, I'm glad I'm not a picture-taker), while Mike and I just hung out. Most of the other guests hit the sauna but, since the idea of rolling around sweaty-like in snow, which is part and parcel of the sauna experience, didn't exactly titillate us, we enthusiastically passed.

We were sacked out by 9 PM. Unfortunately, our snow cave-digging amigos decided to stay up till 11 PM shooting the breeze, despite the fact that everyone at Janet's Cabin is supposed to pipe down between 10 PM and 7 AM. Since they were talking right above us, they kept us awake.

Then, at 6 AM, the Denver group boisterously arose and woke us up. It should be noted that both bad-mannered groups were from Denver, while the quiet, good-mannered groups were from Summit County and Montana. (We just might be able to draw some behavior-oriented inferences here, though, now that I think about it, I seem to remember a few times when it was the Summit County group that was keeping everyone for twelve miles awake, though, of course, I, personally, had nothing to do with those incidents.)

By nine the next morning, after having eaten another atypical backcountry meal (Canadian bacon and eggs), we left Janet's Cabin. Once again, the weather was unbelievably beautiful. It only took us two hours to reach Union Station (we walked all the way down the hill, bypassing the lifts in a most manly fashion).

Within minutes, we were back in civilization. Our return to civilization was so rapid that it almost seemed unreal. But, then again, we had never really left civilization. We had, rather, spent a night at Janet's Cabin.

I don't think I will ever become a backcountry cabin/hut devotee. But, I must admit, the thought of returning to Janet's Cabin, maybe later in the season, when it's not so crowded, with my wife and maybe a nice bottle of wine and some l'amour-ish intentions, has already started to make its way into my thought processes.

It will damned sure never replace camping, but it surely does replace sleeping in my condo in the middle of Frisco for the hundredth straight night.

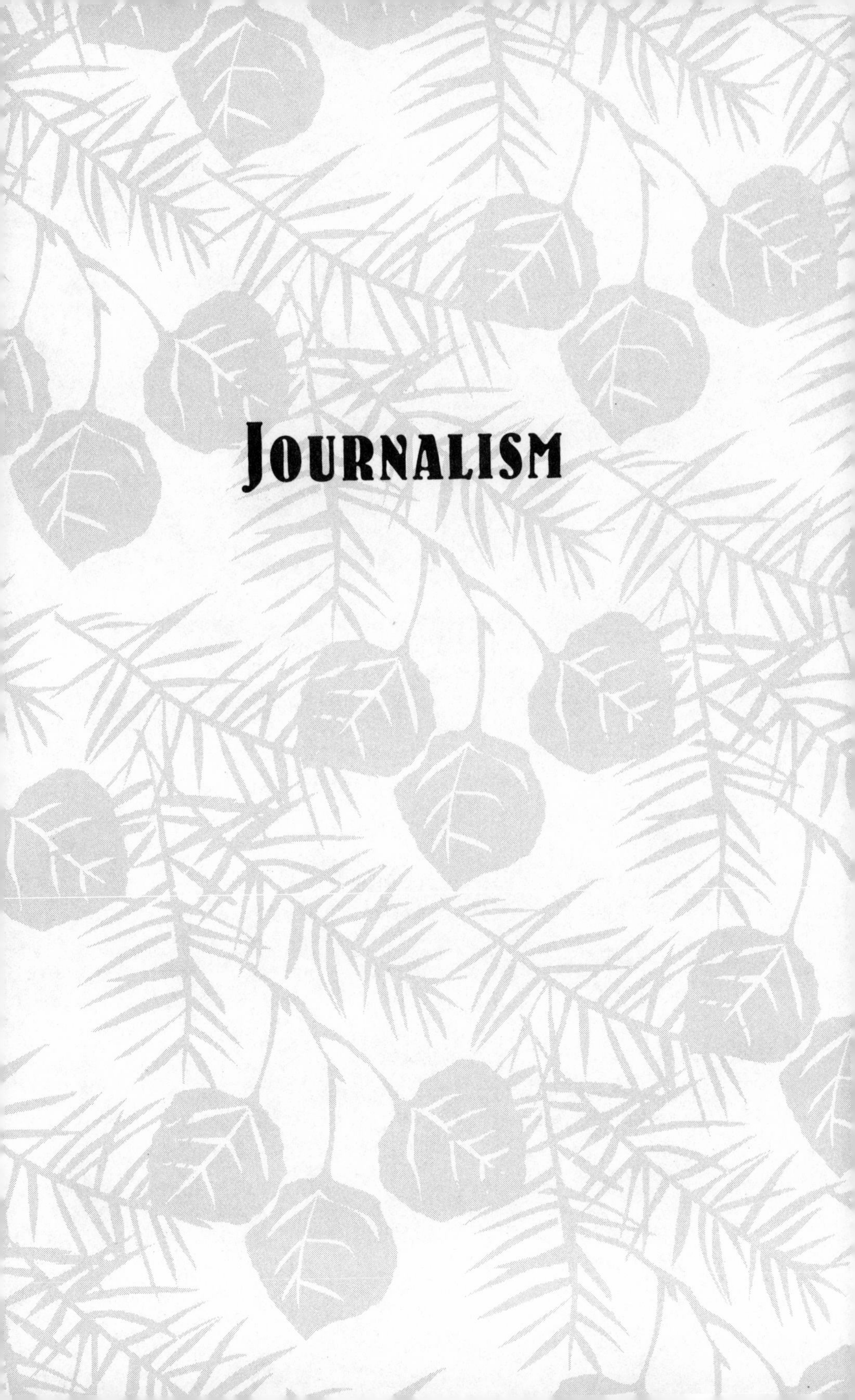

Journalism

The Restoration of Cucumber Gulch

It didn't take Robin Theobald long to notice something fishy. It was 1986, and Breckenridge Ski Area, then owned by Aspen Ski Corporation, had started construction on the Colorado Superchair at the base of Peak 8.

"We noticed problems immediately," Theobald remembers. "I own about one hundred acres at the bottom of Cucumber Gulch, and the runoff from the construction project almost immediately began to affect the water quality on the stream through my property. Though there have been a couple of ownership gaps in between, my family has owned that property since my great-grandfather patented the mining claim on the land. And we've owned it continually for the past thirty years. I know that property very well. I spent a lot of time out there as a kid, and the water was always clear and clean. Then, when construction on the Colorado Superchair began, it turned coffee colored, even during the fall."

Within a year, what had one been a near-pristine, beaver-pond-dominated ecosystem was fast turning into an alpine wasteland. The incredible amount of gravel-laden runoff from the construction at the base of Peak 8, which included putting in a new parking lot, had filled all but two of the dozen or so beaver ponds in Cucumber Gulch, making it impossible for the resident beaver population to survive. Consequently, the erstwhile lush willow bottomland was fast drying out.

By 1988, there were only a couple of beavers left in Cucumber Gulch. Theobald doesn't know whether the rest of the animals moved on or whether they died. Either way, he was one seriously pissed off hombre.

"The runoff from those construction projects negatively impacted my property on several levels," Theobald says. "The wildlife and fisheries habitat that depended on the beaver pond ecosystem was destroyed. The property was less attractive, and the water quality was severely degraded."

Theobald ended up taking Aspen Ski Corporation to court. The end result of that case, which was settled in 1989, is well nigh upon us. And that result is above and beyond anyone's wildest expectations.

After five years of hard work, the beavers are back en masse in Cucumber Gulch, and the ecosystem that Theobald remembers so well is, once more, up and running. It's to the point that you can't even tell there was ever a problem.

But, like many things is the High Country, the more benign they look, the more malignant they seem. At least to some people.

Even though it may have seemed, in the spring of 1986, when Theobald brought suit against the Aspen Ski Corporation, that this was a cut-and-dried matter, when it comes to suing large companies, complexities are the norm.

"To this day, the ski area doesn't admit it did anything wrong," Theobald says. "What was really strange was that the ski area owned, and continues to own, about one hundred acres at the head of Cucumber Gulch. They were ruining their own land, too."

Theobald had to prove that it was runoff from construction at the base of Peak 8 that was killing Cucumber Gulch, and not just some unaccounted-for force of nature. He consulted experts, covering the wildlife and ecology gamut from Division of Wildlife officials to fisheries experts. In just about every one of those conversations, one name kept coming up: Major Boddicker.

"I kept asking people who knew more about beavers than anyone else," Theobald says. "And everyone said the Major."

Boddicker, who had served on the biology faculty of Colorado State University for ten years, was, and is, the owner of Laporte,

Colorado-based Rocky Mountain Wildlife Services, a company that, ironically enough in this context, specializes in helping governmental entities and individuals "deal with" wildlife infestation problems. Boddicker specializes in removing problem populations of prairie dogs, coyotes, mountain lions, and, yes, beavers from ranches, public parks, and private land.

"When Robin first contacted me, we had to determine how we were going to go about assigning blame on this," Boddicker says. "That was the gist of the lawsuit. The ski area at the time was denying that they had even dumped any gravel at the base of Peak 8, yet gravel runoff was one of the biggest causes of the beaver ponds filling in. I had to do a little detective work, but it ended up being a lot easier than I first thought."

Boddicker proved Theobald's case in part by examining the growth rings of Cucumber Gulch's ample willow population. He showed, to the month, that the willows, upon which beavers rely heavily for food, started experiencing diminished growth rates when the construction projects commenced at Peak 8. "It was like a fingerprint at the crime scene," Boddicker says.

In addition, Boddicker started digging into several of the abandoned beaver dams. The evidence he uncovered was, well, damning.

"We found large amounts of gravel of exactly the same type as was being displaced at the base of Peak 8," he says. "And we were talking about hundreds of tons per year coming down Cucumber Gulch. The ecosystem was simply overwhelmed."

The problem, according to Boddicker, was that beaver ponds need to be deep enough that the resident beavers can move under the thick ice in the winter. A certain amount of erosion occurs naturally, of course—meaning that, even without a massive construction project going on upstream, beaver ponds absorb a fair amount of silt. The beavers deal with this by making their dams even higher, which, in turn, makes their ponds deeper. With several hundred tons a year of additional runoff being added to the ecosystem, the beavers could not build their dams up fast enough, and their ponds started filling in, a situation tantamount to a death knell for the beaver population of Cucumber Gulch.

With Boddicker's expert testimony to back up his suit, Theobald was able to reach a settlement with the ski area. One component of that otherwise-undisclosed settlement was a $50,000 sum earmarked for habitat restoration in Cucumber Gulch.

"The ski area was in a position of having to deal with the runoff problem anyhow," Boddicker says. "They were talking about building a $2.5 million concrete retaining pond to catch the runoff. We sold them on this project at least partially because of its cost-effectiveness. We convinced the ski area that, for $50,000 spent over five years, they could take care of their runoff problem and, at the same time, restore the ecosystem of Cucumber Gulch."

Before the project got underway, though, Japanese-owned Victoria USA bought the ski area, and Boddicker and Theobald found themselves suddenly working with different players. They were at least a little apprehensive, after their less-than-totally-positive dealings with Aspen Ski Corporation.

"It turns out that the good guys in all this ended up being from Victoria," Theobald says. "They were in the position of having inherited a problem, but they enthusiastically worked with us in remedying it. They deserve a lot of praise. This is their victory as much as ours."

So, okay, you've got a ski area that's really behind the project, you've got $50,000 to pull the project off, and you've got a guy who everyone thinks knows about as much about beavers as anyone in the state. Now what?

"That was an interesting period," Boddicker recalls. "I walked around the property with Robin a number of times while we were trying to figure out where to start. We knew we had to mitigate the runoff from Peak 8. A healthy beaver pond ecosystem in Cucumber Gulch can certainly handle several tons a year of additional runoff, but not several hundred tons. After the ski area changed hands, they did a much better job of managing their runoff. They black-topped the parking lot and put a lot of effort in revegetation. That gave us a fighting chance."

Boddicker had, over the years, worked around beavers frequently—to the degree that he already had a handle on the needs and wants of beavers.

"When we first began this project, I already knew a great deal about the dynamics of a beaver-dominated ecosystem," Boddicker says. "Also, I had been exchanging information with a man named Gene Smith, who works in the Rock Springs, Wyoming, office of the Bureau of Land Management. He had been working on reestablishing beaver populations on BLM land in Wyoming. I had been helping him in his efforts to live trap beavers and move them safely to areas where he was working, and he helped me by telling me what he knew about establishing artificial feeding programs."

Boddicker and Theobald embarked on a multi-pronged attack. The first plan-of-action was to dig out three of the heavily silted beaver ponds.

"We determined which three ponds had the best shot at being salvaged," Boddicker says. "We made that determination by examining the substrate and the vegetation. Once we determined which three ponds we were going to rehabilitate, we went in with a backhoe and dug them out. We used the silt we removed to help shore up the old dams that were already in place."

The next step was to bring in some beavers.

"That first year, we put seven in, a pair with one baby and two other pairs," Boddicker says. "I even went in and built a lodge out of wire and plastic for one of the pairs, to help them make it through that first winter. "

The final step was to embark on a supplemental feeding program.

"It's kind of like haying horses," Boddicker says. "We would bring in aspen, which the beaver depend on for food and to build their dams and lodges. We also planted a lot of aspen on the side of the gulch but, although some trees are still alive and growing, overall that hasn't worked out too well. We're to the point now where the ecosystem is restored enough that there is an ample supply of willow that is the right age for food."

Boddicker says, once the ponds were dug out, the beaver transplanted in, and the supplemental feeding program established, the restoration project was essentially at the mercy of Mother Nature.

"There was never really a time where I didn't think this would work," Boddicker says. "I just never thought it would work out as well as it did. It was like, all we had to do was give the beavers the chance to reestablish the ecosystem, and they took care of the rest."

After five years of near-constant looking after (Theobald and his family still visit the beaver ponds on their property just about every day), Boddicker's work is just about over. He estimates the Cucumber Gulch beaver population close to forty. And he considers it a very healthy and viable ecosystem. But, he says, in order for it to stay that way, it will have to be manipulated basically forevermore.

"Left alone, beaver ecosystems generally end up going through cycles," Boddicker says. "We have learned through our work here that there have been beavers in Cucumber Gulch for probably ten to twelve thousand years. Yet, there have been cycles. Beavers, like many animals, will overpopulate, and their food supply will become insufficient as a result. And they are very susceptible to outbreaks of disease. So, in order to keep the population stable and healthy, we will harvest about ten to twelve beaver a year from Cucumber Gulch."

"Harvest," in this context, means "trap, kill, and sell the pelt."

So, here I have been walking around Cucumber Gulch with Boddicker and Theobald for the better part of a day, thinking how cool this all is, when, out of the blue, I get told that, in order for this ecosystem restoration project to work, shitloads of cute little beavers have to be killed every year. Suddenly, my brain tosses what my buddy T. Alex Miller would call a mental penalty flag and, equally suddenly, I don't feel so good about what's going on in Cucumber Gulch.

"I know there are a lot of people who will not agree that beavers need to be killed here but, as an expert in this field, I can say it's necessary to maintain the viability of the ecosystem," Boddicker says. "People should understand that beaver populations right now in Colorado are about where they were before the white man came. The state is at its carrying capacity for beaver."

During Boddicker's monologues regarding Cucumber Gulch, he frequently, and quite derisively, mentioned a lady named Sherri Tippie, who has gained a reputation in Colorado for her efforts to save beavers. Boddicker would talk for a while about, say, the need to trap and kill beavers in a small area like Cucumber Gulch, then he would punctuate his point by saying something like, "But, that flake Sherri Tippie would have you believe otherwise."

So, I decided that I had better call Sherri Tippie up to get her opinion about all this.

The first thing you need to know about Sherri Tippie (hell, may be it's the only thing you need to know about her) is that she believes there is no reason whatsoever to ever kill a beaver. And I do mean ever.

Tippie, a Metro Denver resident who had been referred to in the *Rocky Mountain News* as the "Diane Fossey of beavers," has dedicated her life to helping *castor canadensis* survive its inevitable encounters with *home sapiens.*

"There are basically three kinds of negative encounters between beavers and humans," Tippie explains. "The first is where beavers take down trees. The second is where beavers build their dams in places that cause flooding of roads of residences. The third is where a landowner will simply prefer to wipe out a beaver pond ecosystem because he prefers dryer land. All of those instances can be resolved, with a little time and effort, without killing a single beaver."

Tippie, a hairdresser by vocation (she also claims that she used to be the highest paid dancer in Wyoming), got involved in the affairs of beavers in the mid-'80s, when the Denver Department of Parks and Recreation, under the mayoral administration of now-Secretary of Transportation Federico Peña, decided to kill a significant percentage of the beavers inhabiting the banks of the South Platte River Greenway, which passes through the heart of Denver.

"The beavers were taking trees out, and that was causing erosion and diminished aesthetics," Tippie says. "So, they just decided to kill the beaver."

Tippie was incensed by the situation, and she jumped into action like a pack of wolverines on speed. She organized a save-the-beaver campaign, which, first of all, asserted in no uncertain terms that the South Platte's beaver dilemma could be solved by embarking on a program of sterilization and live trapping and relocation and, second, got a serious amount of positive press coverage in Denver.

"I gained my political experiences by working for People for the Ethical Treatment of Animals," Tippie says. "And I have needed all the political savvy I have to defend beavers in Colorado. When I first heard what they were planning to do with the beavers on the South Platte,

I found a study that said beavers could be sterilized. I presented that study to the Colorado Division of Wildlife. They rejected it, and they rejected me. They immediately started making things difficult for me because I was going against policy and history. And that policy and history was based primarily on trapping and killing beavers without batting an eye."

The "history" part Tippie refers to comes from, well, history. Tippie says beavers had more to do with the exploration of the interior of North America than even gold.

"From about 1800 to about 1840, beaver pelts were one of the most-sought-after commodities in the world," she says. "The pelts were used for hats and coats. When white Europeans first came to North America, there were as many as sixty million beaver on the continent. By the mid-1800s, they were almost extinct."

Summit County was actually first visited by white men because of its beaver population. According to local historian Mary Ellen Gilliland, between 1810 and 1840 (several decades before the county's famed mining era kicked in), when beaver pelt hats were all the fashion rage, about the only white faces one would stumble upon in these parts belonged to beaver trappers. Since the beaver of the High Country produce particularly luxurious pelts, they were highly prized and, according to Gilliland, the local beaver population really took it on the chin as a result.

Tippie adds that beavers also got into trouble because of their busy-as-a-beaver-ness. "Beavers are one of the few animals that can significantly manipulate their surrounding ecosystems," she says. "That seems to bother a lot of people, but, the truth of the matter is, that manipulation is very important to the natural world."

In addition to her support of using birth control methods for "problem" beavers (they are live-trapped, anesthetized, sterilized via Norplant contraceptive implants, tubal ligations, or vasectomies, and released back into the wild), Tippie says that relocating troublesome beavers is a perfect solution.

"First of all, I need to point out that there is no market whatsoever for beaver products," she says. "I have been working for a decade now on live trapping and relocating beavers. The process of live trapping a beaver, certainly, is more time-consuming and difficult than using traps that kill the beaver. But, it's also worth the effort. I've transplanted God knows how many beavers in the past ten years, and I always manage to find a place for them. Anyone who says Colorado is at a saturation point with beavers doesn't know what they're talking about."

When I told Tippie about my time spent in the field with Boddicker, she near-bouts went ballistic. To say that she hates Boddicker's goddamned guts is a severe understatement.

"He's a good ol' boy from the old school," she says. "He's one of those people who believes there's no wildlife conflict that can't be resolved by killing animals. If he managed to live trap beavers to bring up to Cucumber Gulch, then he can damned well live trap beavers and move them elsewhere if there's an overcrowding problem up there. And, if he can't, I will."

In order to institutionalize her beaver-protecting/saving efforts, Tipple helped organize Wildlife 2000, a non-profit animal rights group based in Denver. As president of Wildlife 2000, which counts about four hundred members, Tippie spends most of her time traveling around the Rockies preaching the gospel of beaver preservation.

"I spend most of my time live trapping and relocating beavers, as well as trying to convince people inclined to kill beavers for whatever reason that there are workable alternatives," she says. "I also give a lot of talks. The thing is, I was raised in the '60s, but I'm not a pacifist. I go toe-to-toe with people, and beavers are important enough to me and to the natural world to do that as often as necessary."

At least partially because of Tippie's efforts, beaver populations in North America have now reached about twelve million—the highest level in more than a century.

"We'll never get to a point where there are as many beavers as there were, mainly because of a loss of habitat," Tippie says. "But, we're finally getting to a point where people concerned with the survival of beavers can start breathing a little easier."

Back to Cucumber Gulch. After five years of work, Boddicker is a mighty proud man. As he walks around what is once again an obviously vibrant ecosystem, he can scarcely keep from grinning.

"I've learned a lot here," he says. "The major thing is I've learned how predictable this was and how well it worked. It's nice to be able to throw an idea like this out, but it's another thing entirely to see the project completed even better than you predicted. I mean, I'm not a fruitcake-type person. I knew this was going to work. And, now, I can prove it. The other thing I learned is that this is an easily replicable type of project. It has applicability to other areas that have been degraded."

Both Theobald and Boddicker believe that the restored ecosystem in Cucumber Gulch offers a lot of benefits.

"There's a value that can't just be measured in dollars and cents," Theobald says. "The wildlife and fisheries habitat has been improved. It's prettier to look at than it was, and the fish grow faster than they would if there were no beaver ponds in here. The thing I really like about this project is that we dealt with a problem—severe runoff—in a completely natural fashion. It proves we don't always have to deal with impactful projects with other impactful projects. This has worked out better than I could have imagined."

"The chief value I see in a functional beaver pond ecosystem is the increased water quality," Boddicker says. "The recirculation of the water throughout the system improves the quality of the water significantly. It also cuts down on potential flooding. It is an ecosystem that stores nutrients very efficiently, making it very attractive to all sorts of wildlife, including deer and elk. Certainly, a beaver pond ecosystem has its drawbacks. There is an increased bug problem because the area is so wet. And some people just don't like all the water. A lot of people prefer valleys that are dry and grazeable. But, all in all, I think this is a very valuable asset to the county, and I'm really pleased with the work we've done here."

Overall, it sounds like there is potential for some common-ground dialogue between Theobald/Boddicker and Tippie. But, they are simply different kinds of people. Though they both love wildlife and the land, they can't agree on how it should be managed. It is a situation that seems too typical of the kinds of conflicts that frequently dominate the High Country landscape. In a place as special as this, common ground should be the easiest kind of ground to find. But, oftentimes, it is as scarce as cheap housing in a ski county.

Gold Fever

The history of the West is steeped in gold. And gold itself is both heated passion and cold science—the blistering desert sun yin-and-yanging with the frigid waters of a mountain stream. It has brought religious ecstasy at the same time that it has caused severe environmental degradation, at the same time that it has caused heinous crimes to be committed against individuals and groups of individuals.

That's because gold is so damned valuable. It is not money; it is what money pretends to be. It is functionally the jock strap of our world economy. But, if we are able to keep things in a reasonable perspective, the casual/recreational seeking of gold offers potential riches far beyond just getting one's covetous mitts on a few small pieces of heavy yellow metal—especially in a gold-rich place like the High Country.

Seeking gold affords the opportunity to meet and talk to prospectors and hard rock miners—living remnants of a bygone era that the children of Nintendo can reach out and touch and shoot the bull with. It gives us the opportunity to expand our understanding of the natural world, for without that understanding, you will find no gold. It can help us become sun-tanned, with muscular forearms, for the effort of seeking gold is physically demanding. And, when you get right down to it, if your Karmic ducks are in a huddle and you combine a little enlightenment with a lot of luck, seeking gold could even add a tad to your bank account.

My personal love affair with gold-seeking began about thirteen years ago down in the arid wastes of southwestern New Mexico. I was working for a daily newspaper and was, as usual, scrambling around hoping against hope that a good story would walk up and kick me in the ass. I'd heard about this absolutely nuts barroom preacher/old-time prospector who lived hermit-like in a shack way out in the remote (even by southwestern New Mexico standards) Burro Mountains. I'd also heard his shack was quite possibly sitting atop one of the richest veins of gold ever to be located in those parts.

So, I sought the man out. What I found was both a literal and figurative gold mine.

I met Jack Kiesling, who has since passed away, one Christmas Day. I pulled up to a friend's apartment on my motorcycle, and the first thing I saw sitting out front was this grizzled old character who looked like something out of an antique photo. Before we even exchanged pleasantries, he handed me a quart Mason jar filled with what looked to be lemonade. I got it as far as my lips before recoiling aggressively from the smell. It wasn't lemonade. I handed it back without even tasting it, which is saying something, as I do not often back off from beverages just because they are so damned skanky smelling they make me want to run screaming through the night.

"You younguns ain't got no sense of adventure nowadays," Kiesling said, cackling. Then he proceeded to suck down half the contents of that jar without batting an eye.

"This stuff is so watery it hardly deserves to be called moonshine," he snorted.

He estimated that it was only about 120 proof. I asked if he did his own moonshine-making.

"Only enough to see me through the year," he answered. "I only drink about a quart a day, so I don't need to make much. My needs are modest."

Kiesling, who was banged up pretty badly at the time (he had been thrown off a bridge after getting his butt kicked in a bar fight, which ended up breaking some ribs and fracturing his pelvis), essentially became my gold-panning mentor. We ended up hanging out quite a bit for the better part of a summer. He was so eccentric that he was essentially shunned by most people with any sense in that part of the state. I think he just liked having someone to talk to.

When I say Kiesling was eccentric, perhaps I am extending unnecessary politeness toward the dearly departed. Kiesling was as whacko as anyone I have ever met. The name of his mine was "Jacob's Promise," and that name did not come about by accident. Kiesling was the son of a prospector and had grown up chasing what he called the "yellow metal that drives the white man crazy." His father, true to the ardent prospector stereotype, moved around a lot, mostly in the Sierra Nevada.

Thus, Kiesling grew up with, to say the least, a working knowledge of gold-related geology, to say nothing of the gold-related lifestyle. Somewhere along the line—and he was always a little hazy on this—Kiesling got married, had a passel of kids, and apparently settled down for a while. It didn't last long. His addiction to gold-seeking eventually caused the demise of his family life.

Not long after his wife left him, Kiesling was diagnosed as having inoperable throat cancer. He was given six months to live. One night, he had a dream/vision sort of thing—which, as much as anything, serves as notice to any note-taking reporter that, perhaps, now is a good as time as any to start putting the notebook away whilst looking for a mannerly excuse to takes one's leave.

But, hell, the story was compelling enough, and I have never held it to a person that they need to tell me the truth, as long as they package their stories interestingly.

In his vision, Kiesling was visited by the prophet Jacob, who told him that, if he were to move to the Burro Mountains, he would be drawn to a very rich gold mine. Kiesling was instructed by Jacob to patent the mine, to move onto the property, and to start digging like crazy. Kiesling was told that the mine would produce incredible wealth that should be used to help the homeless. (This was several years before the concept of homelessness really made its way into the national headlines.)

He was further told that, if he did all these things, his cancer would be cured. The mine was to be named Jacob's Promise. Kiesling did all he was asked and, by his word, his cancer had indeed gone away. The only problem was that the mine proved to be not only a dud, but the kind of dud that makes for mirthful storytelling on the part of other prospectors for miles around.

After my first couple of interviews with Kiesling, I realized that our conversations had been, up to that point, very theoretical in nature. He told me stories about his hits and misses in the world of gold-seeking. He told me, for instance, about the one "glory hole" he found. In one small crevasse in a small California creek, Kiesling said he pulled out $10,000 worth of nuggets. He said he managed to spend every cent in six weeks, but, he acknowledged, those were some mighty interesting six weeks.

He staggered out of town drunk and broke and headed back to that same creek with high hopes. But he never did find another hole like that.

However, despite this plethora of bullshit, I had yet to actually lay eyes on any gold. Then, one day, I took Kiesling to breakfast at Dollie's Cafe in Silver City. Suddenly, right there across the stained Formica table, Kiesling pulled out a vial of gold and proceeded to attempt to pay for his huevos and coffee with a few of the flakes. Miss Dolly shook her head, telling Kiesling that she couldn't accept as payment gold that "ain't been assayed yet." Miss Dolly always did have high standards.

I must admit, there is a certain human interest quotient that is part and parcel to seeing someone attempt a business transaction, even a modest one, using gold flakes. It was a captivating experience, after which Kiesling and I would often go panning along the Big Ditch in downtown Silver City in the early mornings, he sipping moonshine, me smoking weed.

It was under such circumstances that I panned out my first "colors"—little, teensy, itty-bitty pieces of gold grains visible only by holding the pan up in the sun and using a magnifying glass. But, those small grains of gold glimmered against the black dirt in my pan like a visual equivalent of the "Hallelujah Chorus." Remember Bogey in

The Treasure of the Sierra Madre? That was me: my eyes narrowed, my five-o'clock shadow instantly darkened, and I got ready to stake out all of Silver City as my claim.

Kiesling just sat there drawing on his hand-rolled cigarette with a wry grin on his sun-scorched face. I could tell he thought those grains of gold in my pan were "cute."

"You are now in possession of the most addictive substance known to man," Kiesling said.

The High Country is a hotbed of both serious and recreational gold panning. Every weekend, you can find dozens and dozens of people panning for gold near Central City and Blackhawk (where the first Colorado gold rush commenced in 1859), in Clear Creek County, near Fairplay and, to a lesser extent, in Summit County, especially up French Gulch.

Seeking gold seems to be locked into the genes of Colorado. In the minds of many people is the historic knowledge that an awful lot of gold has been taken out of the streams of this state. When you understand that the most often-stated prospector's adage is, "To find gold, look where it's been found already," you can understand what makes the lure of the yellow metal that drives the white man crazy so irresistible for folks in these parts.

It is impossible to even guess the number of active gold panners in the U.S., because there's no national entity that keeps count. Some impressive statistics have been collected on the local level, however.

"We have more than 650 members just in our local amateur prospectors club," Charlie Brown, former owner of the Gold Prospector's Shack in Glendale, Arizona, told me by phone. "That's a ten-fold increase in five years. And there are lots and lots of clubs in the West. We're not even the only one in the Phoenix area."

Adds Gary Christopher, owner of the Prospector's Cache in Englewood, "Gold panning is hot, and it's getting hotter by the day. We have been in business almost fifteen years, and business gets better every year. I would guess that at least ten new people a week come in during the spring and summer looking to buy their first panning gear."

While prospectors at every level of expertise admit (how could they not?) that the prime reason for the rebirth of recreational panning is the not-so-inconsequential price of gold (between $350 and $400 per troy ounce), most add that there are many adjunct reasons.

Says Brown, "People are more outdoors-oriented these days. The problem is, sometimes when you're just camping, you can get bored. So, people are looking for ways to amuse themselves while they're outside. Some take up photography, some take up flyfishing. A lot of people take up gold panning because it's so easy to combine with other outdoor activities. It's potentially profitable, and the whole family can enjoy it."

Denver resident John Donahoe, who was seventy when I met him panning along the South Platte near Fairplay a few years ago, had only recently taken up panning.

"I was always an avid hiker," he says. "But I'm getting too old to hike much. I wanted to take up a hobby where I could still see the mountain views. I've always been sort of an armchair geologist. Gold panning gives me an opportunity to use my knowledge. I've found a few hundred dollars worth of gold, and that's a big thrill, of course. But, it's just one part of the reason for doing it. The rest has to do with being outside, enjoying nature."

Jessie Peterson, a Blackhawk resident who has been giving gold panning lessons on Clear Creek forever, puts the gold panning phenomenon into a sociological context: "The myth of gold panning in the American West is very strong. It speaks of a free and independent lifestyle with no traffic jams or mortgage payments. I believe there are an awful lot of people who are bored with life. Gold panning adds excitement to life—especially if you find gold."

Peterson is one of the few prospector-types I have ever met who can rank up with Kiesling on the eccentricity scale. It's almost like there's a prospecting college somewhere, and each of them graduated with honors after having done so well in Image 401 and 402.

Peterson moved up to the North Fork of Clear Creek in the mid-seventies with little more than the shirt on his back. He seeks gold primarily because he likes the freedom of the lifestyle. He ||works only for himself, and he isn't paid from a computer with eight different deductions taken out. His fringe benefits are wind, sun, cold, and gold.

Within a half an hour after I first met Peterson, I held in my hands two things that most people will never see close-up in their entire lives, except maybe in a museum.

The first was something that most folks would have no desire to ever hold: a Russian-made machine gun, capable of blasting out something on the order of 1,200 rounds per minute. Peterson invited me to come back sometime later in the summer, after his seasonal supply of ammunition arrived from California, to "shoot some trees down." (I ended up being *very* busy that summer and never took advantage of the invite.)

The second item Peterson handed to me—and one that would probably be received a little more readily by your average, say, suburbanite—was a one-and-a-quarter-ounce, solid gold nugget.

By weight alone, that nugget would be worth well more than $500. But, to a collector, the price would be many times more, nuggets of that size being pretty rare and all. He pulled it out of Clear Creek and, from what I was told by folks in-the-know around Blackhawk and Central City, it was the largest chunk of gold to be pulled out of those parts in decades.

Just the thought of a nugget that size sends shivers down the spine of anyone who's ever pretended to hunt for gold. And the thought of actually possessing it makes you wonder just how far you could go if it ever got right down to it. Whereas the thought of committing foul play in the name of money has never crossed my mind (except while playing poker with my lying, cheating amigos, of course), as I was sitting there with a loaded Russian machine gun across my lap with Peterson opening his safe, exposing even more—thousands and thousands of dollars more—gold, I noticed sweat beginning to form on my trigger finger.

"Don't worry," I told him, "I'll make sure I won't ever write anything about all this gold being here in your cabin."

"Why would you worry about a thing like that?" he asked.

"Well, I thought you might be a little leery about having people learn that you have so much gold stashed here . . ."

"First of all," he said. "if someone was to steal my gold, I'd just have to go out and dig some more. But, I don't know too many people crazy enough to come in here after my gold." The look in his eye seemed to say that he almost wishes someone would try. The machine gun is only one of the serious weapons he keeps around. And, with two years in the marines under his belt, I get the feeling he knows exactly how to use them all. And when. The rest of us would scurry on down with all that gold to the closest safety deposit box and pass on the responsibility of protecting our valuable possessions to someone else.

Gold panning, not surprisingly, is not like buying a lottery ticket, where you figure, if you buy enough of them, you're bound to win, sooner or later. Gold panning forces you to learn about the physical peculiarities of a metal that's 1.9 times heavier than pure iron, itself a very heavy metal.

You can pan till hell freezes over and, if you never bothered to learn anything about gold's wicked habits, you'd do better to just stick with the lottery—if quick fortune is your goal. The only way an ignorant gold panning rookie would ever stumble across gold would be for the Great Mother Lode in the Sky to stick it in his or her pan personally.

Most panners agree that the best way to get started is to hook up with someone who already knows what they're doing—like I did with Jack Kiesling down in New Mexico. Fortunately, finding a seasoned professional is fairly easy. Just about any notable gold-mining area boasts a cadre of prospectors who have learned that it is much gentler on the back muscles to prospect for tourists by offering panning lessons than to actually look for gold itself.

There are several places right along the Peak-to-Peak Highway in Gilpin County, for instance, that offer panning lessons. But, the aspiring panner needs to beware. For, though it takes but a few hours to learn the basics of panning, you could spend the rest of your life mastering the intricacies of searching for gold.

"Gold occurs only in certain places," Peterson once told me. "And you need to learn what those places look like. Even then, there's no guarantee you'll find gold. There are no guarantees at all when it comes to looking for gold."

Mary Tiefert, a Denver resident I met panning on Clear Creek a few years back, suggests that novices begin their gold-panning education by joining a prospector's club, where they can learn from a variety of experienced gold-seekers.

"I went on a trip to Alaska that was sponsored by a treasure-hunters club," she told me. "The people were the most interesting I have ever met. They were glad to show me what they knew. And that included so much more than gold panning. There were people who knew all about the cultural history of the area. There was one guy who was a serious birder. One man was a professional geologist. I learned more about the natural world in two weeks than I had learned in the previous forty years.

"I really enjoyed learning how to look for gold," Tiefert continues. "Now, I spend most of my free time, including vacations, panning. I have purchased a metal detector and a small dredge and sluice box. I would really like to get good enough to make my living prospecting."

Tiefert's relatively quick transition from raw beginner to would-be professional is not all that unusual, according to Brown.

"I would estimate that 50 percent of the people I deal with take the next step up from just owning the basic panning equipment—which can be purchased for under $25—and eventually buy a dredge and sluice box," Brown says. "That means they have made the decision to get a little more serious about looking for gold. Even though it's cheap to get into panning at the beginners level, like many things, it costs more to get into it more."

But, many people are making that decision these days.

Because, as one man told me on the bank of the North Fork of Clear Creek, "The more gold I find, the more excited I get."

I know what he means. After more than a decade of panning, I have reached the point of having a small plastic vial almost a quarter of the way full with gold. Maybe, by the time I am fifty-seven, I'll have enough to get a tooth crowned. That's a pretty exciting thought. But even more exciting is the notion that, by the time I reach that age, maybe my bullshitting abilities will be as well developed as Jack Kiesling's. Now that would be something.

The Bud Girls

When the Bud Girls walk into a bar—any bar—time freezes on the half shell. Jaws drop. Mouthfuls of carbonated beverages instantly become active ingredients of aggressively discharged drool compounds. Lecherous glares dominate the male facial landscape. These are ladies who are seemingly designed from the DNA level on up to command attention when they make their appearances.

This attention-commanding was highly apparent when two Bud Girls from Denver, "Venus" ("Like the planet," she explained, just in case we mixed her name up with the flytrap) and "Dayna" ("With a Y," she stressed. "Why?" I asked. "Because," she answered.) spent a few hours at Eric's Underworld in Breckenridge one December evening a few winters back.

Even though Eric's Underworld (which Eric has since sold) does not exactly suffer from a dearth of eminently observable young ladies, when the Bud Girls are on the scene, they *are* the scene. Just about every other female in the bar finds herself taking a back seat when it comes to being part of any sort of l'amour epicenter, even if, point-two seconds before, that's exactly what she was.

This should come as no surprise, as the Bud Girls are vocationally trained, to say nothing of dispositionally oriented, to be the life of the party. They could liven up a Rotary Club meeting (and they probably should).

At the same time, the Bud Girls do not exactly dress demurely. At the same time, the Bud Girls are not exactly grotesque to look at. ("Easy on the eye" was the term used by a table of young gentlemen from Nebraska who were sitting close to us, and I tended to agree with that assessment.)

Several dozen times each year, Summit County watering holes host events that include appearances by the "Bud Girls." I have long wanted to interface journalistically with the Bud Girls during one of their Summit County visitations. So, when I learned that there would be a Bud Girl promotion at Eric's, photographer Mark Fox and I decided to set up an interview with them.

They were late enough that we became at least slightly concerned we had either screwed up the day we were supposed to meet them, or else, mayhaps, they had entered the bar surreptitiously without our noticing them, which would have been hard, as we were sitting as close to the entrance as people can sit. And, we were keeping our eyes peeled for anyone who would even remotely resembled a marketing component of the world's largest brewer of beer which, coincidentally, happens to be my beverage of choice.

When Venus and Dayna (they are not allowed to give their real names, out of justifiable security concerns) finally did arrive, we laughed at the thought that they could have cruised by us without being observed and immediately vocationally identified.

Dayna stood well over six feet tall. She had a blond bouffant that could have earned her membership in a B-52s clone club. And she was one of those ladies whose legs go all the way up to her shoulders.

Venus was a doe-eyed goddess. Her lipstick was so perfectly applied that it looked as though she had spent the entire previous week with a Hollywood makeup artist. I mean, most women, even those who put lipstick on daily, usually have a teensy little smudge that passes past the lip boundary on its way up towards the realm of the nose. Or else there's evidence of uneven application, where the lipstick is thicker on one lip quadrant than it is on another, or something. But, not Venus. Her makeup, from soup-to-nuts, was as tasteful and perfect as any makeup ensemble I have ever seen.

There's a good chance I would have proposed to Venus right on the spot, except for the fact that my wife was sitting about six inches to my starboard as my fluttering heart was melting directly down my aorta like a newly loosened Drain-O clog making its way down a rusty pipe—during which time, because of spousal considerations, I am trying to act innocent and disinterested, like, "Oh, hell, the crap you've gotta put up with when you're a writer."

Then, to top things off, both Venus and Dayna were wearing black Ice Beer mini-dresses that, in lesser fashion circles could well be described as slightly longer-than-usual T-shirts. These wonderful, wonderful garments were so tight it seemed improbable that anyone, even lithe young ladies like Dayna and Venus, would be able to slip into them without serious assistance from someone like, as a random example, me. (It should be noted here that the Bud Girls have three different guises: Bud Girls, Bud Light Girls, and Ice Girls. Even when they are attired in Ice Beer dresses, they are still known as "Bud Girls.")

According to Venus and Dayna, being a Bud Girl is a part-time position, usually taking up three nights a week, but sometimes taking as many as five nights a week. In addition to her Bud Girl gig, Dayna works in Denver as a model and a bartender. Venus works in Denver selling jewelry. Both are employed by Clear Creek Distributing of Idaho Springs, which is the exclusive distributor of Anheuser-Busch products in Summit County.

"I got the job a year ago by answering a newspaper ad," Venus says. "The ad said they were looking for someone with energy and personality, and that's pretty much how I describe myself. They also wanted people who were intelligent."

"I heard about the job last August through one of the modeling agencies I work for," Dayna says. "Like Venus said, they were looking for someone with a very high energy level. It was also important, I was told, that whoever was hired was willing and able to learn all about the products we represent. We have to know all about the brewing processes for Bud, Bud Light, and Ice. If anyone asks us any questions about those products, we need to be able to answer them."

This would probably be a good time to delve into the Bud Girls' actual job descriptions.

"We are supposed to generate enthusiasm for our products," Dayna says. "There are several ways we go about that. The most common way is to move from table to table, just talking to people. If they are drinking one of our products, we thank them, and ask them what they like about those products. If they are drinking products from another company, we ask them if they would like to try a Bud, Bud Light, or Ice. We tell them all about our products, and, hopefully, they will change their drinking habits."

The main marketing tactic the Bud Girls use is personal contact. And, in this, they are experts. During the half-hour or so I interviewed Dayna and Venus, both maintained the kind of locked-in focus on, in this case, me, that can only be achieved by someone trained, experienced, and intuitive in the art of making the person upon whom their attentions are focused feel like he/she is the center of the universe. In thirty minutes of talking, neither Venus nor Dayna let their eye contact with me waiver for even a second. They did not once gaze bored-like around the room. Neither did they fidget, scratch, yawn, belch or, for that matter, blink. (I like to think that this degree of attention stemmed from the fact that I am such an intriguing person; but, in a retrospect enhanced by input from my wife, I have come to the conclusion that such was probably not the case, and that in all likelihood, I was just another in a long line of poorly dressed, High Country-dwelling pendéjos that the Bud Girls have to pretend are worth a few minutes of feigned enamor. Que lastima!) Then, the exact instant the interview was over, they thanked me profusely for my time and interest and commenced to wade neck-deep into the teeming masses of Eric's Underworld.

It was very interesting to see them in action. As the Clear Creek people were keeping them under close scrutiny, they made their way, just as advertised, from table to table. They always moved as a team and, just like during my interview with them, they made the people they were hobnobbing with at any given moment the absolute focus of their attention.

Of course, at most of the tables they visited, they were greeted cordially by normal-enough-looking folks who were made mirthful by a Bud Girl visitation. There was gentle, smile-dominated breeze-shooting for a few minutes, then Venus and Dayna would move on to the next table. But, at a few of the tables, especially the one behind us populated by the boys from Nebraska, rubbing elbows with a pair of

Bud Girls seemed like the biggest event in their lives since that big corn harvest three years ago.

There was hootin' and hollerin' and various politically incorrect descriptions containing words like "little filly." Then there was some photo-taking with one of those cardboard cameras, "just so's everyone back home will believe this, because, without pictures, they won't." And, all in all, it was a real fun time, for the boys from Nebraska, for the normal folks at Eric's Underworld, for the Bud Girls, and for us.

With any sort of marketing/promotions job, there is certainly going to be a heapin' helpin' of mouthing the company line, which is sort of what the definition of marketing/promotions jobs is. And, certainly, during their interview with me and during their table-to-table forays, Venus and Dayna, safely hidden behind their noms de beer and their Bud Girl costumes, tow the Anheuser-Busch company line with aplomb. Only once during my interview did that company line-towing seem to make them uncomfortable. As tactfully as I could, I asked a question that begs asking: what, if anything, does being a Bud Girl lead up to? Which, after all, is a valid enough question because, it would seem from the sidelines, being a Bud Girl does not exactly seem like a career-track job.

I was wondering if Venus and Dayna were hoping to use their Bud Girl exposure as springboards to careers in acting or increased modeling opportunities or whatever.

They both glanced (I thought somewhat nervously) at each other and said basically the same thing: being a Bud Girl is a very fun job that offers up lots of valuable experience that has the potential to transfer to any number of other kinds of employment, like, well, marketing and promotions and PR work.

Fair enough, at least partially because it doesn't matter one iota if being a Bud Girl is a stepping stone to something bigger and better or if it is a dead-end part-time gig like any other dead-end part-time gig. Dayna and Venus say they are enjoying themselves and they appear to be doing just that. They seem to be providing a valuable service to their employers. And the recipients of that service, bar patrons and people attending special events all over the High Country, seem to enjoy the company of the Bud Girls.

If only every component of life could be so symbiotically positive. It is enough to make a man want to sit in a smoky bar with a Bud in-hand while talking, even if only for a few seconds, with a beautiful, scantily attired young lady whose job it is to make you feel like the center of the universe. There are certainly worse things.

Note: I rubbed elbows with the Bud Girls twice more after interviewing them. The first time was in Barkley's Margaritagrille in Frisco. Venus and another Bud Girl were on the scene participating in a promotional evening very much like the one at Eric's Underworld. I didn't talk with the other Bud Girl, but Venus came over and chatted for a while. She was feeling lousy, but still had to keep a smile on her face, even though it was clear that she should have been home in bed neck-deep in a nose-blow-a-thon . . .

Then, a month later, I was watching the Ullr Fest Parade in downtown Breckenridge. It was about 4 PM in the middle of January, and it was well below zero. After several dozen of the silly kinds of floats that dominate the Ullr Fest Parade (which is part of week-long Ullr Fest, an event designed to celebrate, worship, and appease the Norse God of Snow) went by, a convertible made its way down the street. Sitting in the back seat were Venus and Dayna, scantily attired as ever, smiling and waving, representing their products very well in the middle of the frigid High Country winter.

Made me want to consume a Bud.

One-hundred-day Skiers

It is a cliché that is really not so clichéish: The vast majority of people who live in the High Country ski less than a lot of people who live in, say, Denver. Most of us moved here for the skiing and, maybe during our first few seasons here, we managed to hit the slopes with due diligence and reasonable frequency. But, after several years, even the slackest of us ends up embarrassingly gainfully employed—which means more cash and vocational stability, certainly. But, it also means less time on the slopes.

Some people, though, have either made lifestyle decisions that still allow them to ski many, many, many times a season, or they have forgone any thought of gainful employment whatsoever, living an austere existence solely for the sake of the skiing life. Others have "real" jobs that simply take place during surreal times of day, meaning the daylight hours are available for turning and burning down the slopes. Still others placate their need to ski by actually working on the slopes as ski patrollers or ski school instructors.

At the summit of the skiing fanatic mountain dwell the high priests and priestesses of the alpine kingdom: those who have done whatever it is they have to do to ski almost every day. These are the one-hundred-day-per-season-plus skiers.

These are people who would rather ski than, literally, do anything else in the world. They are focused, intense, and jovial about their lifestyles. They count themselves not so much among the lucky as they do among the sane. And they look at the rest of us, those who only ski a few times a year because of work and/or laziness constraints, as genetically inferior to whatever degree, on whatever level or levels.

Herein we visit with five one-hundred-day-per-season-plus skiers. Call it a lesson in gray reality.

Bruce Ruff

Age: Thirty-five. Lives in: Frisco, in a two-bedroom condo at Mountainside. How many years skiing? Since age six. Employment: Manager of Mountainside. Favorite place to ski: Slalom Slope, A-Basin, Prima Pronto, Vail, Resolution Bowl, Copper Mountain, North Peak, and the Outback, Keystone. Average number of days skied per season: About 120.

Bruce Ruff, like most one-hundred-day-plus skiers, almost bump-skied his way out of the womb. He grew up in upstate New York and skied, along with his family, the various areas in the Catskills, Adirondacks, and New England—especially Sugarloaf Mountain, Maine. He learned to ski from his father, who was a seventy- and ninety-meter ski jumper and a competitor in Nordic combined.

He attended Cortland State, in New York, where he majored in physical education. While in college, he was a member of the Cortland ski team. He also taught skiing part-time at Song Mountain while going to school.

"While I was in college, I skied just about every day of the season," Ruff says.

He is, was, and will always be, first and foremost, a bump skier.

"It was my fantasy while I was in college to ski the Pro Mogul Tour," he says. "I only taught phys-ed for one year. That was back in the days when teachers made $9,000 a year. That wasn't enough to support my ski habit. So, I moved out here fifteen years ago to find a way to ski on the tour. I was on the tour for fourteen years, until 1992, when I blew my ACL out."

In fourteen seasons on the tour, Ruff always maintained a full-time job. He fared well over the years, taking a few thirds. But, he only competed in the Colorado and Utah events. It simply was not cost-effective to travel with the tour.

In the world of one-hundred-day skiers, Ruff operates as much in the mainstream as a person possibly can.

"I am the resident manager of a condo complex with over two hundred units, plus I have waited tables quite a bit," he says. "I work very hard. And, consequently, I need a release which, for me, is skiing. I really like the bumps, because I consider them to be the ultimate skiing challenge. I love being out in the fresh air doing something athletic. Skiing is a total release from everyday life."

Though Ruff has a real job and a stable, even sorta regular, lifestyle, he admits that, to be a one-hundred-day skier, one has to make sacrifices.

"I don't have the chance to work on poetry or to work on my art during the ski season," he says. "You basically ski, work, and sleep."

Ruff is in the process of working out a way to be paid for skiing.

"Right now, I've started a company called Ad Ski," Ruff says. "I wear a ski suit advertising Barkley's Margaritagrille in Frisco. They bought me a Ski the Summit Pass and the suit. I'd like to get to the point that I'm doing a lot of on-slope ad work. After all, I'm out on the slopes almost every day. I'm a good advertising deal."

Ruff says the key to being able to ski one-hundred-plus times a season lies in enlightened moderation.

"I won't ski eight hours a day anymore," he says. "I'll ski from, say, noon till three. But, I ski so hard I exhaust myself. I've fully recovered from my ACL injury, though I do wear a brace now. I want to still be doing this, still leading this lifestyle, at sixty-five or seventy. I'll have to let up on the bumps at some point. But, that's okay, as long as I can keep skiing every day."

During the off-season, Ruff, like all one-hundred-day skiers, doesn't exactly take it easy.

"I rollerblade a lot," he says. "I do a lot of mountain biking and I lift weights. Though I really enjoy doing all of those things, skiing is always in the back of my mind. And, as soon as the snow starts falling in October, I'm one of the first ones out."

Wendy Sorcic

Age: Thirty-one. Lives in: Leadville, in a two-bedroom house she owns, along with her husband, Dennis. How many years skiing? Since age three. Employment: Five shifts a week as a waitress at the Funhog Ranch in Silverthorne. Favorite place to ski: Anywhere in the Summit will do. Average number of days skied per season: 100–110.

When it comes to a good skiing-oriented upbringing, Wendy Sorcic struck gold. The younger sister of Bruce Ruff, Sorcic had the opportunity to ski with three older brothers, all of whom were serious about their schussing.

"My brothers were real encouraging," Sorcic says. "If I ever whined, though, they would tell me I had to ski with the boys or ski alone. Now, the boys ski with me."

Like her brother, Sorcic, who has been married five years, cut her teeth on the icy slopes of the Northeast. She attended Cortland State and majored in physical education. During her student teaching days, though, she determined she didn't like kids.

So, she bought a round-trip ticket to Colorado to visit her brother, forewarning her parents that she could be gone for anywhere from two weeks to forever. That was in 1983.

"For me, life revolves around play," Sorcic says. "My husband doesn't necessarily like to hear me say that, but that's because he works during the day and can't ski as much as me. He's a real good skier, and he's jealous. I work to pay for my toys, but I work five shifts a week and that's enough. Usually in a relationship, one person gets to play more. It's not my fault that it turned out to be me."

Sorcic says one of the biggest problems in developing her professional play-oriented lifestyle was fending off parental admonishments for her to do otherwise.

"For several years, my parents would ask me when I was going to use my degree and get a real job," she says. "My dad would ask me about my plans for retirement. They stopped shaking their heads when I called them up to say I had started a retirement account. I'm happy to report that I also have a checking account, a savings account, and health insurance."

Sorcic says she is attracted to skiing on every level one can possibly be attracted to skiing.

"I really love the thrill of going fast," she says. "I like pushing myself and trying to get better and better. Even as much as I ski and as long as I have been skiing, there's still room to improve. Always room to improve."

While not skiing, Sorcic enjoys macramé, listening to opera, and puttering in the garden. Right.

In truth, Sorcic is, not surprisingly, a serious body nazi. Even during those rare winter days when she's not on the slopes, she bikes like a madwoman.

"Yeah, I try to get over one thousand miles in on my bike every year," she says. "I rode nine miles in the snow yesterday. I also ice and rock climb, play hockey, soccer, and lacrosse. And, of course, there has to be time for kayaking."

Like her brother before her, Sorcic says she will continue down the road of play-oriented life forevermore.

"This is my life," she says. "I can't imagine anything else. As long as I am physically capable to keep going, I will keep going. I've stayed healthy so far. I've never been hurt. I have great knees and a strong back."

Mic Fairchild

Age: "Between thirty-five and forty." Lives in: A town south of Boulder—Eldorado Springs, in a mobile home that's bought and paid for. How many years skiing? Since age fourteen. Employment: Works at a grocery store three days a week; teaches rock climbing in summer. Favorite place to ski: Anywhere there are trees, in legal out-of-bounds areas at Breckenridge and A-Basin, North Color of Torreys Peak. Average number of days skied per season: 100.

It would be tough to burn it at both ends any more than Mic Fairchild. In addition to skiing as many as one hundred days per season while living and working on the Front Range, Fairchild climbs rock as many as 150 times a year, mainly at Eldorado Canyon.

This is a man dedicated, on a cranial as well as a physical level, to the sports he loves. And he lets nothing, save the very occasional injury, get between him and the deep powder of Summit County.

Fairchild didn't begin skiing until he was fourteen. He was living in his native southern California and was invited one day by some neighbors to join them on a ski foray to the Sierras. He was promised by the parents of those friends that, if he could pull off a stem Christie by the end of the first day, they would buy him a pair of high-fashion sunglasses. He went home with a brand-new pair of high-fashion sunglasses.

"We rode up to the mountains in a Porsche," Fairchild says." It seemed appropriate."

Though Fairchild attended college in California, where he majored in journalism, there was no doubt that he was psychically Colorado-bound sooner or later.

"I left on a trip that took me to L.A., Key West, and, finally, to Denver, where I knew some people," he says. "This was in 1974. I liked Colorado and ended up just staying. I knew I was addicted to skiing by then, because the year before, I had bought my first season pass, which was good at thirteen different areas in California. I had Vail season passes in 1974 and 1975. In '76 and '77, I had season passes at A-Basin. In '79, I had a season pass at Copper. I've had twelve Ski the Summit Passes. I bought one the very first year they came out, and I've had them ever since."

During his early years in Colorado, Fairchild, who has arm muscles on top of his arm muscles, actually worked a succession of surprisingly regular jobs, including managing a Dave Cook's sporting goods outlet in Denver and doing a computer systems gig in Golden. During those dark years of regular employment, Fairchild still managed to ski an average of seventy days a season.

But, he was locked into a four-day work week and that meant missing good powder too many times.

"The work schedule I have now allows me to be very flexible, and that's important if you are serious about your skiing," he says. "If you can only ski on certain days of the week, you miss a lot of good snow, because it doesn't just snow on your days off. My work now keeps the bills paid, and my trailer is paid for. This lifestyle definitely affects the finances. I have to shop for bargains on ski equipment. Even though I own twelve pairs of skis, each for different conditions, I can't afford to buy the newest gear every season. You also have to keep your debt down to a minimum. You have to order your priorities."

Those priorities include not only financial considerations.

"My type of lifestyle definitely has an effect on relationships with women," he says. "It's cost me a few girlfriends."

Fairchild is drawn to the snowy mountains for many reasons.

"I've gotten to the point now where I don't have to concentrate so much while I'm skiing," he says. "I'm good enough that I can count the number of turns I missed during the course of a ski day. I am able to simply let go mentally while I'm skiing and that is very relaxing. I love the quiescence of the sport. I also love the feeling at the end of the ski day. It's a good tired."

Fairchild feels that, in order to be a good skier, one has to be a versatile athlete.

"I climb a lot, mainly because it's a good opportunity to see women in tights," he says. "But, more than that, climbing is good for the attitude, and it's good for strength. It makes the body more aware. I also mountain bike a lot, because it keeps the legs and wind in good shape."

Like most other one-hundred-day skiers, Fairchild plans on keeping on keeping on until he can no longer, well, keep on.

"I've been pretty lucky in that I've only had one severe injury in about two thousand ski days," he says. "Last year, I busted some ribs and was out for ten weeks, during which time I mainly thought about what an idiot I was for getting hurt. The thing is, though, I'm a better skier now than I was ten years ago. I've been active in the summer and going nutso in the winter since 1974. The pace has been sustained at the expense of everything else. But, I don't see an end in sight. It's just a matter now of picking my spots and skiing smart. If it wasn't for skiing, I'd be just another $50,000, sixty-hour statistic."

Dave Cook

Age: Thirty-three. Lives in: Silverthorne, in a house with six other people. How many years skiing? Since age six. Employment: Works five to seven nights a week as a ski tuner for Virgin Islands Ski Shop. Works as a carpenter during the summer. Favorite place to ski: Just about anywhere, but really likes the north chutes of Buffalo Mountain. Average number of days skied per season: 150–200.

To Dave Cook, there is simply no other alternative. Life is meant to be spent in the pursuit of skiing as many days as humanly possible every year. But this striving for numbers does not necessarily do Cook's attitude towards skiing any justice. It makes it sound like he is the skiing equivalent of a long-distance runner, racking up days instead of miles in his quest for something the rest of us mortals can't quite figure out.

Nothing could be further from the truth. Cook skis so many days simply because he skis, and wants to ski, every damned day of the year. As long as there's snow on the ground somewhere, Cook will find it, even if it means hiking to some remote snowfield at 13,000 feet in July for a ten-second descent through mostly dirt and rock.

"You could say I'm addicted to it," Cook understates. "But, it's a good addiction. I simply love skiing. I'm one of those who wish ski season lasted all year. One year, I went to Australia for the summer. The day I got off the plane, I was skiing. I ended up skiing over three hundred days that year. That was a good year."

Cook hails from San Diego. He embarked on a fairly normal educational pathway, attending the American Academy of Art in Chicago, where he studied photography. After graduation, he took what has to this day turned out to be the only "real" job he has ever had.

"I worked in a sweatshop, taking pictures for Sears catalogues," he says. "I hated it. I came out here in 1980 for a vacation. Two weeks later, I quit my job and moved out here. My parents hated it. At first they thought it was something I would probably grow out of. But, by now, they've just given up and they accept the lifestyle decision I have made."

And, with Cook, "lifestyle decision" is a vast understatement. He says he is willing to do anything necessary to keep himself on the slopes every day.

"The feeling of freedom I get from skiing includes more than the act of skiing," he says. "It's the whole lifestyle thing. I am totally debt-free. I cut up my credit cards four years ago. I own my vehicle. I just get by with money, but that doesn't bother me at all. You definitely sacrifice creature comforts when you live like I live."

To say there are many things that attract Cook to the slopes is yet another understatement.

"I like scaring the you-know-what out of myself," he says. "I like skiing faster and faster and getting bigger and bigger air. I'm always looking for something steeper and steeper. There's almost nothing I won't try to ski. It's not just that I'm a little crazy. I also happen to be a very good skier. I also like the camaraderie part of skiing. Some of the best friends I have ever made have been through skiing."

Cook plans to stick with some variation of the lifestyle theme he has been living for the past twelve years.

"Even if something happened where I couldn't ski anymore, I'd still live the way I do," he says. "I've already had reconstructive surgery on one knee, so it's conceivable that my body won't hold up forever. But, if I had to stop skiing, I still wouldn't become just another clone in the big industrial machine, because, before you know it, you're in so deep you can never get out. If I had to give up skiing, I'd probably move to Hawaii and take up windsurfing."

In the meantime, Cook has two immediate goals. One is to move out of his current domicile. At the end of the month, he plans to take up residence in his camper van for the next few months to save sanity and money.

Second, he wants to buy a lot where he can build a cabin. Can total responsibility be far behind?

Brian York

Age: Twenty-nine. Lives in: Keystone, in a duplex, with one other roommate. How many years skiing? Since age thirteen. Employment: Waits tables four or five nights a week at Bandito's and teaches skiing at A-Basin three days a week; works as a carpenter during the summer. Favorite place to ski: A-Basin. Average number of days skied per season: 130.

There is one sin above all others to Brian York: to sleep in on a powder day.

"Can you imagine anyone doing that?" he asks, incredulously. "I know people who will either be too tired or lazy or they have to do laundry or something and they'll blow off a powder day. I'd never consider doing that."

This attitude was born and raised, like York, in Allentown, Pennsylvania. Like many one-hundred-day skiers before him, he started down a normal path, before seeing the light before it was too late. He attended Kutztown State College for two and one-half years, where he studied studio TV production. Then fate intervened in a very strange way.

"I got hit by a car," York says, grinning. "We settled out of court. I soon dropped out of college and moved to Colorado for three months. I've been here for nine years and haven't really thought about leaving."

York skis because he loves the outdoors and being healthy.

"I love the freedom you feel in the mountains," he says. "I love the beauty. I love the clean, fresh air, the exercise, and the fact that it's good for you. Of course, I'm also addicted to the adrenaline component. Going fast is fun."

The two main problems York sees with living the one-hundred-day life are fundamental problems, indeed.

"First, you either have to have a very understanding girlfriend, or no girlfriend at all," he says. "They've got to understand, when they want to snuggle in front of the fire when it's snowing, that you're going to be out on the slopes. The other problem is finding the right job. You've got to be able to have your days off."

York had been skiing, for the past seven years, on the Pro Mogul Tour. He retired this year, at least partially because of health concerns.

"I wasn't having any problems," he says, "but I wanted to keep it that way. So, I cut my hair and started teaching at A-Basin. That way, I'm out on the slopes and getting paid for it three days a week. On my days off, I ski."

York says he works hard during the off-season, which, for him, lasts about nine seconds, to stay in shape for skiing.

"I ride my butt off on my bike all summer," he says. "I really like riding, but the main reason I do it, or at least the main reason I do so much of it, is to stay in shape for ski season."

In addition to riding his butt off this summer, York has one other serious off-season goal: to buy a car.

"Right now, I can walk to the slopes, but I'd still like to get a car someday soon," he says.

Winter on the Ranch

Winter is the quiet time of year for the Grady Culbreath family and their Otter Creek Ranch. Most of the thousand or so head of cattle they ran on their 1,200-acre spread last summer have long been sold. Sure, there are chores that need doing. But mostly those are relatively little things, especially when compared to the raucous pace of ranch life that dominates the rest of the year.

"There's really not much to do right now," Grady Culbreath says over a cup of coffee in the kitchen of his one-hundred-year-old house, located at the base of the Gore Range, a couple miles outside of Heeney, in the lower Blue River valley. "Things really start picking up in February, when we start getting our herd for the year. Right after that, calving season starts, and that's a time of year when you don't get too much sleep. It gets you out of bed in the middle of the night knowing that, if you lose a calf, you've just lost $500."

What there is to do in the winter for Grady Culbreath is contemplate life. And, when he does that, there's a good deal of smiling, head scratching, and thankfulness. Because, even though, as a third-generation High Country rancher, Culbreath has rubbed elbows in a big way with the vagaries and vexations of ranch life, all in all, he thinks he's been about as lucky in life as anyone has a right to be.

He's got four kids and four grandkids. (Another son passed away last year.) He's got some of the best views in the High Country right out his back door. He gets to spend a lot of time outside. He is happy, and he is tranquil. And, as one of the few ranchers left in a part of the county that was, as little as thirty years ago, dominated by ranching, Culbreath is one of the few voices left that can speak to the "way things were" out where the views open up so wide you can almost see Wyoming out there over the endless sage-dominated vistas.

Culbreath, though clearly a man who does not dwell much on the past, feels strongly that we would all do well to think a little more about the "way things were," if for no other reason than to help map out the future of a place that is clearly wrestling with its own identity and direction as the new century looms before us like a gaping, carnivorous, greed-infested maw.

Grady Culbreath has lived just about all of his fifty-eight years in the lower Blue River valley.

"My granddad came out here and homesteaded near Kremmling with his two brothers in the 1870s," Culbreath says. "He ran a saloon in Breckenridge, and then he ran a bank in Breck. That bank foreclosed on Otter Creek Ranch, and my granddad bought it. My folks ended up buying him out. I bought them out."

Culbreath attended a one-room elementary school near Heeney, Colorado.

"It was amazing how many little houses there were in Summit County back in those days." he says. "I went to high school in Breckenridge. That was before the new high school was built in Frisco and, to tell you the truth, I don't remember if it was called Summit High or Breckenridge High at the time."

Either way, after graduating from high school, Culbreath left the ranch for a total of six-and-a-half years, not only the longest stint he was ever away, but the only stint.

"I went to Colorado State University in Fort Collins, where I graduated with a degree in animal sciences," he says. "Then I was in the air force for two-and-a-half years, during which time I was stationed in Denver, Washington, D.C., and the Philippines. By the time I was in the air force, I was married to my wife, Gail, whose maiden name was Byers. She was from a long-time Summit County ranching family, too. We knew we would always come back here. I had made a deal while

I was still in high school to start buying the ranch from my father."

When Culbreath returned to Summit County in the '60s, ranching was the dominant industry in the lower Blue valley.

"I would guess there were at least thirty-five or forty families around here making their living ranching," he says. "Most of those were small operations, and a lot of people spent a lot of years barely getting by. But cattle provided a strong economic base, and it provided a lot of jobs. I really think the county was better off then, because it seems like families were stronger, and the bonds of the community seemed stronger. Unfortunately, things started getting tough in the '60s, and a lot of people had to get out of the business, or else they had to sell their land and go to work for someone else."

These days, Culbreath guesstimates that there are only four or so families that still own and operate their own ranches in the lower Blue valley.

"There are still other ranches operating," he says, "but they are owned by absentee landlords. It's not the same thing. There's no doubt that the boom in tourism, which really got going in the '60s, had a lot to do with the decline in the ranching industry. It just got so the land was far more valuable as resort property than it ever was as ranching property. That's just the way things work."

But, that situation, in an ironic twist of fate, has worked to the benefit of the Culbreath family.

"The value of land in Summit County has allowed us to stay in business," he says. "We have sold off a few parcels over the years and made good money off those sales. If we lived in a place where land values were low, it would have been hard to make it. I sometimes don't know how ranchers stay in business in other parts of the country, where land values are very low. I have a daughter and son-in-law who ranch up in Wyoming. They got their land for very cheap. But, it's hard up there, and they don't really have the option of selling their land off at a profit if things get too tough."

The fact that the Culbreaths have had to sell 432 acres of their land over the years has certainly had one palpable consequence: their current spread is simply not large enough to support the kids and grandkids.

"It used to be that a family ranch could perhaps support the kids, but no longer," Culbreath says. "Ranching families have to disperse.

I have one brother who owns a ranch near here. There was just no way we could both work Otter Creek Ranch and make a living."

Even though Culbreath's Otter Creek Ranch is substantial and profitable, Culbreath has always had to rely upon other sources of income to get by.

"For a long time, we've leased the ranch to hunters during hunting season," he says. "We have an amazing elk population here. Sometimes, we have literally hundreds of elk grazing on our land. The hunters love it, and we make a little money from them. We've also sold gravel, and we've traded land for other parcels. It's definitely been a lifetime of creative financing. "

The elk situation Culbreath faces is yet another example of the ironies of ranch life in Summit County.

"The entire ranching industry, along with the timber and mining industries, is really on the defensive right now," Culbreath says. "The environmentalists, most of whom know absolutely nothing about agriculture, accuse us of being in a business that is detrimental to the environment. That's just crazy. First of all, we have a sense of stewardship for our land that is the most important thing in our lives. But, more than that, we are currently supporting a large number of elk in Summit County. So are all the ranchers. The grass that the elk eat is not owned by the government; it's our grass. That's money out of our pockets. Yet, when we talk about wanting to graze our cattle on the public lands, we get accused of being welfare ranchers.

"The whole system right now is being run by people who have no idea what ag's all about," Culbreath continues. "I grew up feeling good about what I do, about the fact that we can take a non-usable resource, like grass, and turn it into food. Things have changed. Now, a lot of people don't look at it that way, although they don't seem to mind eating beef."

The burning question regarding the ranching life is simple, yet compelling: Why? If the business is tough, if the public relations quotient of that business is low, why continue? Why put up with the long hours, hard work, and the crap? With 1,200 acres of prime real estate in the nation's largest ski county, wouldn't it simply be easier to sell the land and retire to some nice, warm place, like, say, the Pacific coast of Mexico?

"We couldn't bring ourselves to move away from here," Culbreath says. "We love it too much. We're part of this land, and it's part of us. When I was gone away in the air force, all Gail and I thought about was moving back to the ranch. It's who we are. It's what we are. I have one son whose ashes are spread on this property. The ashes of both my parents are spread out here. I've had two daughters who were married here. We've simply got too much of ourselves wrapped up in this place."

It's easy to see how that could be. In addition to having one of the nicest pieces of property in the county, the Culbreaths boast one sweet domicile, which includes a sun room and a hot tub.

"Things weren't always this comfortable," Culbreath says, with a wry grin. "When I was growing up here, we didn't have electricity. We had a phone, but it didn't work all the time. We didn't have a TV, only a radio. It was a very isolated life. It was tough. What makes this place so beautiful also makes it hard to run cattle. Running cattle in a place with winters as harsh as ours is not easy. We used to keep our herd all year, but that got to be too much. So, we sell most of the herd every year in the fall. We keep a few head until after the first of the year, for tax purposes.

"We've stayed with this because we've always loved this life," Culbreath continues. "It's really been challenging to adapt ourselves to all the changes we've seen. And it's been a goal of ours to keep this land, no matter what. There are a lot of people who would pay a lot of money to have what we have, to see what we see every day of our lives. We're smart enough to appreciate what we've got. And we're dedicated enough to this land and this lifestyle to want our children to have this place when we pass on. That's very important to us. Our grandchildren are fifth-generation Summit County ranchers, and we happen to think that's pretty special."

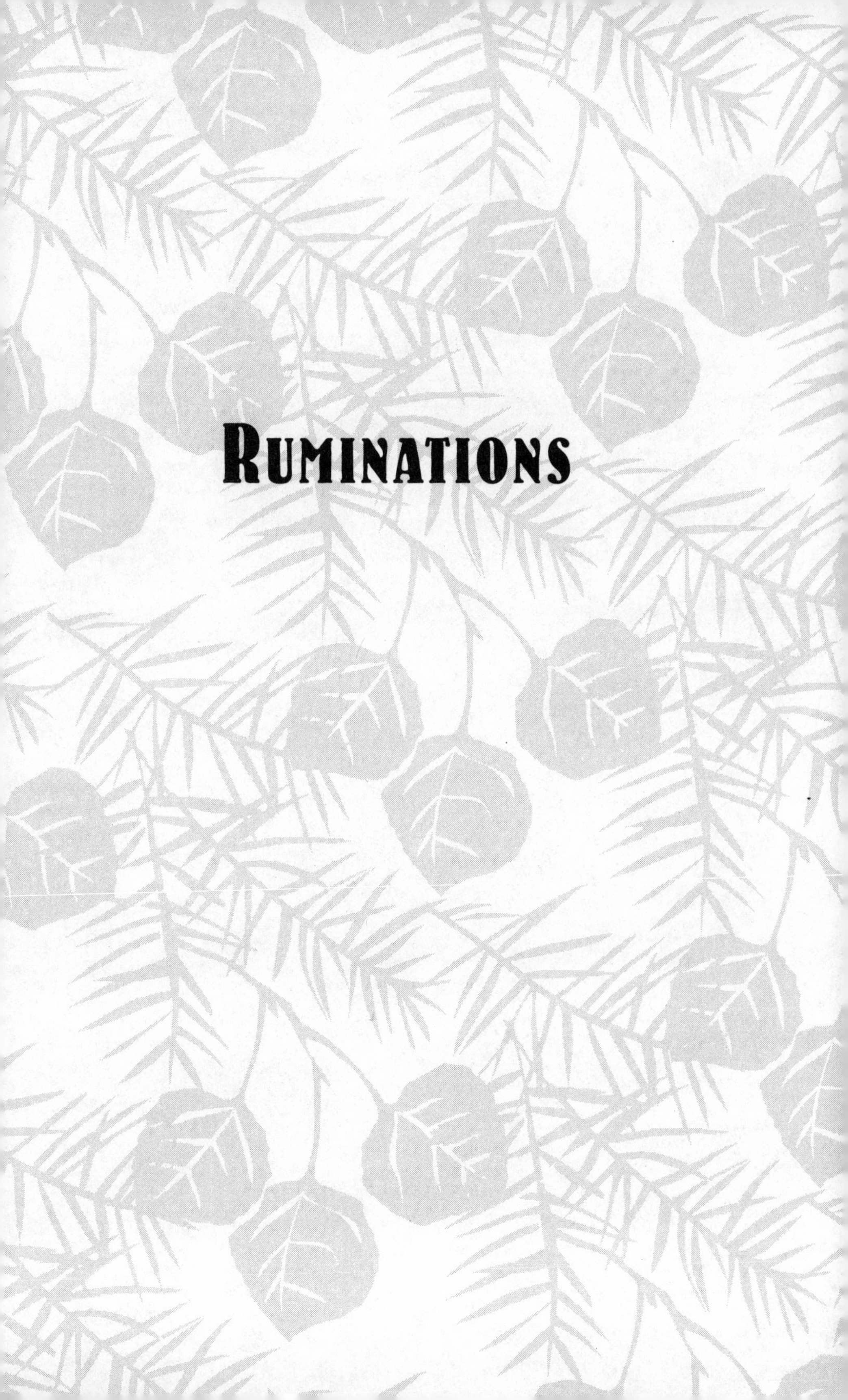

RUMINATIONS

Company Loves Misery

In the dialectic pantheon of the High Country, few words, besides maybe "eviction" and "DUI," carry a wider array of mutually understood connotations, denotations, and oh-my-God-not-again-notations than "company." This one little word has so many meanings, cross-meanings, and multiple-meanings that, by merely repeating it in the presence of any other single member of our species, you speak volumes.

For instance, there you are leaning on a poorly cleaned bar with several empty—and several full—Bud longnecks before you, with a glaze over your eyes that can best be described as indicating an ongoing psychic wrestling match between suicide and murder, and someone you have never met in your entire life can waltz in and, in doing nothing more than exchanging greetings, ask how you're doing.

All you need to say is "company," and with those seven, seemingly innocuous letters, you have spoken a High Country version of *War and Peace*, *Roots*, and *The Oldest Living Confederate Widow Tells All*, all in one fell swoop.

You just said, with that one word, that your life has been turned on its ass-end and that what little inner peace and tranquillity you have managed to maintain throughout the course of a long winter has been fed a handful of amphetamines and is now ready to wreak havoc and mayhem upon mankind. You have told this perfect stranger that you now have no more beer and bread in your house, that all of your cassettes have been strewn upon your now-filthy carpet, that you have been kept awake with inane chatter until midnight for three straight nights, and that all your towels are dirty. Not that the latter point matters much, because you haven't had a drop of hot water come your way for several days since you have fallen to the bottom of the ladder when it comes to shower availability in your own home.

Unfortunately, when you live in the High Country, you are a perfect target for the kinds of people who have no problems whatsoever with being called "company." I must confess, I have never been partial to receiving company. There are many reasons for this.

First, I dwell in a fairly small two-bedroom place. Since our second bedroom is used for an office, we have no guest room. Any company we have is particularly intrusive due to nothing more than space limitations. Two extra people sleeping on your floor means a minimum of two more times you're going to be awakened in the middle of the night when they get up to take a leak.

Next, company, no matter who, always ends up costing money. Even if it's just via an extra fourteen showers per day of hot water, it adds up. But, the costs of company are never measured merely in gallons of hot water pouring down the economic drain of life. You'll always end up feeding them somewhere along the line, and certainly buying them beers. We have considered charging company a flat lodging rate, like some of my friends, but have never figured out a mannerly way to bring the subject up. And, even when it comes to company, I'm still a stickler for manners.

Then you have the terminal boredom factor. Your personal company might actually be fairly together and interesting but, let's face it, a certain percentage of anybody's company is going to take the form of people you have nothing whatsoever in common with.

Now, I know this sounds like I am implying that all company is unwanted, that the people who come to sleep on High Country sofas and floors are across-the-board blighted by all manner of social mutancy. Not necessarily so. There are always ex-college roommates and ex-lovers and friends from high school and well-loved siblings. But, unfortunately, no matter who these people are, and no matter the place they hold in your heart, in your past, or in your DNA, these people will always still be company. Before they arrive, they are company, meaning you have to clean up the place, go out and buy more groceries than usual, and pick them up at the airport on a Friday night instead of relaxing over a few cold brewskis with the people who matter most in your life *now*.

When they are here, they are company, meaning all of the things we have already talked about come to pass, combined with a few other things I have neglected to mention because the memories are too painful. And, long after they are gone, they remain company, meaning you are now going back to square one, because you have more company coming next week.

Just about every person who works where I work gets infected by the company virus at least once a winter. There have been in-laws, out-laws, ninth cousins, ex-girlfriends, some of who are now married to someone else, even relatives of ex-girlfriends, ex-roommates we didn't even like while we were roommates and, worst of all, people whom we still like but who were in the midst of a six-month trip around the country, meaning we felt, the whole time they were here, like crap because we weren't in the middle of a six-month trip around the country.

Sad to say, if there is one thing about company, it's that practice does not make perfect. It's a hopeless situation. We have even considered leaving town whenever company is coming. You know, "The key is under the doormat, have a nice stay." But, why should we have to hit the road simply because of company? That's the ultimate visitation impact.

We have talked about instigating certain company rules. For instance, people can only stay for two nights and we are not going to spend a dime on them while they're here, maybe not even allow them to get up in the middle of the night to take a leak. Until we institutionalize all this though, at least we have the benefit of knowing that mud season is almost here. Even company is not stupid enough to come here then.

True (Mostly) Confessions of a Midnight Rambler

There is a chilling madness to the pre-dawn hours. It is a madness I have always enjoyed rubbing elbows with and being part of. Sad to say, though, the older I get, the less and less that elbow-rubbing takes place. It is to the point where my relationship with those pre-dawn hours—which used to be a huge part of my life—exists primarily in memory. Though the scale of the comparison is way off, of course, it is probably how Hemingway felt in his later years about Spain and bullfighting, like maybe you're not even remembering your past, but someone else's.

While I was in college in southwestern New Mexico, I was awake and at least moderately operational between 3 and 6 AM at least three times a week. I always sashayed into the pre-dawn hours from the front end—meaning I did not rise from my slumber early to face the dawn but, rather, I stayed up all night.

For some reason, perhaps caused by an over-emphasis at the time on the writings, musings, and lifestyle mythology of Hunter Thompson, I was under the impression that the only time of day that the muse visited the writer was while the rest of the world was visiting the Land of Nod. In recent years, I have occasionally gotten up at 5:30 AM or so to do something stupid and uncreative like working out or going to the airport to pick up some ne'er-do-well amigo, but the pre-dawn hours are no longer a part of my life, except that, technically,

I am not dead during them; it only appears that way. I no longer stay up all night writing or walking around town or listening to tapes at a high volume or talking with other deranged English majors about Blake, which was always pretty funny, because none of us ever understood Blake, though we pretended we did.

I don't miss all that enough to attempt to re-create the ofttimes all-night lifestyle but, nonetheless, I do miss it enough to miss it.

Not long ago, I was presented with the opportunity to once again slow dance with the pre-dawn hours. Our main delivery person at the newspaper where I work was going on vacation and needed someone to fill in for him for twelve working days. This would entail getting up by at least 2:20 AM and delivering the paper in Frisco, Dillon, Keystone, and Silverthorne. All told, roughly five hours of cruising through the High Country while the High Country sleeps.

I ran with it. Or, better stated, I drove with it—bleary-eyed.

Though I often used to be awake during the wee hours of the night, only twice before have I ever worked between midnight and dawn, that time of day referred to by workers, in tones that border between reverence and disdain, as the "graveyard shift."

In the summer of 1980, I was a watchman on the steamer *Delta Queen*, which cruised up and down the Mississippi River. My duties included strolling around the boat from 10 PM till 6 AM, checking things out, making certain there were no fires, all the while visiting whatever members of the crew happened to be hosting late night/early morning social gatherings in their quarters. I took that job fairly seriously because if the boat ever did catch on fire, everyone was depending on me to sound the alarm before any passengers got toasted.

The next year, I worked on a juvenile-rehabilitation-company-run wagon train. Every two weeks or so, each staff person was required to maintain "night watch," which meant you stayed up all night sitting around the campfire, making certain none of the cute little criminal tikes under our jurisdiction escaped into the darkness. At least one staff person, some years before I went to work for the company, was killed by several kids making the great escape in the middle of the night. Consequently, I took that job fairly seriously, too.

I can't honestly say that delivering newspapers around the county rates quite as high on the seriousness scale as my two previous graveyard shifts but, hell, when you work all day trying to churn out a rag that has at least some redeeming social values, you want to make certain it gets out on the streets sometime on at least the right day.

The first thing you come to understand about a place that flat-out boogies for most of the day is that this is one seriously quiet place after bar closing time. New Orleans this ain't. This quietude is a great thing when (1) you're delivering papers, and (2) you really enjoy the feeling of—for lack of a better way to put it—the anarchy that comes hand-in-hand with empty streets. Now, this is not to say that I feel that a feeling of anarchy *only* exists while streets are empty, or that even the best anarchistic feeling can occur only when you're by your lonesome at 3 AM on Main Street, America. The true anarchist revels in his/her beliefs and actions in the bright light of day, right under the nose of officialdom.

That might be the case, but that attitude taken to its logical extreme would surely result in many more traffic citations than I would like to own. You see, when I talk about a "feeling of anarchy" in the pre-dawn madness, I'm talking about an ability to drive like an absolute madman with little or no chance of being handcuffed and thrown into jail.

During the white sanity of daytime, I might as well be a little old lady when it comes to driving. I obey speed limits and use turn signals and always stay buckled up, even when I'm sitting in a fast food restaurant parking lot eating a burger and reading the sports section. But, this has a lot more to do with a desire to not rub elbows with the judicial system than it does with any belief that things like speed limits are worth a damn.

My wife believes I was born for but one purpose in life: to drive in Mexico. Because there are very few policemen between Mexican towns, the open road is just that—open. Once I cross the border, I become a character straight out of *The Road Warrior,* except that I still just go ahead and obtain my gasoline the regular, boring way.

While delivering papers in the deadest of night, I could pretend that I was in Mexico—driving at illegal rates of speed up the wrong side of the road with headlights off, not using turn signals, pulling high-G-force U-turns going the wrong way up one-way streets, the whole crazy shebang. What coolness.

Of course, that coolness is also dangerous as all get-out. Which, when you get right down to it, is maybe something one should not embrace as enthusiastically as I obviously embrace it. Because, after all, there is a reason why most people are dead asleep during this time of day. Biorhythmically, humans are designed and manufactured to crash out during the pre-dawn hours. And, just because you're out and about and supposedly functioning at 4 AM doesn't mean your inner being isn't thinking mighty hard about lying down for a snooze, even when you're driving at 70 mph down the Dam Road, headlights out, taking advantage of the big moon, rather than lying on your bed. But, hell, what does the inner being know?

The other reason that driving like an idiot late at night is not so, well, smart is that, for reasons that I have never heard explained satisfactorily, humans tend to hallucinate at that time period that borders 4 AM. No matter how intellectually you try to tell yourself that there really isn't a person walking alongside the road just outside your peripheral vision, this is a hard argument to believe, even though it is you making it to yourself, a person who should be inclined to believe you.

All in all, I really enjoyed reconnecting with a time of day that used to be my main time of day, but, man, things change. I couldn't wait for our delivery guy to get back from vacation. Maybe it was because, after delivering papers, I had to work a regular work day. Maybe it was because I didn't have anyone with me to talk about Blake. Whatever. My reconnection to the chilling madness of the pre-dawn hours is now another thing of my past.

It was cool while it lasted because you face yourself when it's 3 AM and you've got your truck door open with Midnight Oil blasting and echoing through the nooks and crannies of your hometown, all the while wondering if you're waking anyone up, who'll lay there wondering who on earth is out at this time of day, thinking whoever it is must be nuts to be out and about while the rest of the world is snoring.

He Who Dies with the Most Toys Maybe Just Withers Away

The older I get, the less I seem to be able to make time in my day-to-day life to get out and about in the hills for more than two or three hours at a time. When I was in my early twenties, living in southwestern New Mexico, I averaged two nights a week sleeping on the ground. That's more than one hundred nights a year sitting around the campfire smoking horribly cheap cigars, looking up for hours on end at the stars, taking extreme liberties with flatulence, and generally rubbing elbows with the backcountry in the ways young men (along with the occasional young lady) ought to rub elbows with the backcountry.

The fact that I camp probably about twenty or thirty nights a year these days ought not, in and of itself, be cause for a midlife-crisis type of concern. That's still more nights than your average human camps and, besides, when one starts getting older, things, you know, change. One simply has less time to get out in the woods for more than an afternoon trail run or mountain bike ride.

I'm getting increasingly uncomfortable with those excuses, though—for several reasons. First, even though I camp less than a third of the nights I used to camp, I own more in the way of camping paraphernalia than I ever could have imagined back when I was in college. Hannibal had less camping gear when he crossed the Alps than I have in my closet. And that seems significant.

Back in my camping heyday days of yore, I owned one of just about everything I needed. I had a backpack, tent, stove, cook kit, rain gear, sleeping bag, and boots. And I generally tried to buy the best gear I could afford and, when stuff wore out or got stolen, I replaced it ASAP, often at the expense of things like rent and tuition. But, I possessed very little beyond those basic necessities. Why on earth would I have wanted more than that? Rather than spending money on more gear, I would spend money using the gear.

Now, I own two of everything, and three of many things. I have two backpacks, two summit packs and a fanny pack, three tents, a bivvy sack, three stoves, two Therm-A-Rest pads, two complete sets of raingear, two water filters, several pairs of boots and trail shoes, and—get this—a Coleman lantern.

Now to defend myself at least a little, neither simple greed nor increased income are the only culprits here. These days I have a wife, and that requires more in the way of outdoor equipment than you might think, because if the wife is not comfortable and happy, then the husband is not comfortable and happy. As well, I have made my living on and off over the years guiding people into the backcountry of Mexico's Copper Canyon, meaning I have had to possess enough in the way of extra stuff to handle the needs of several other folks, as well as myself and the Tarahumara Indian guides I hire. Also, since I do a lot of writing for outdoor magazines, I've received more than my fair share of free demo gear from manufacturers.

But the fact remains, if I spent half the money I have spent in the past three years on camping gear, I could have afforded twice as many camping trips. And that seems, at a minimum, boneheaded and, at a maximum, symptomatic of a deteriorating set of values and priorities.

Back in the late '70s and early '80s, I would just up and leave on an overnighter at the drop of a hat. The reasoning was simple enough: (1) I lived very close to some mighty fine camping turf, and (2) I loved camping; therefore, I ought to get my butt out in that turf as often and as long as possible, lest I offend the backpacking gods.

Even if I had an 8 AM class, I would leave town just before dark, drive fifteen miles up to the Little Cherry Creek Campground in the Gila National Forest and just spend the night out under the stars, sometimes alone, sometimes with the entire cheerleading squad of Western New Mexico University. (Right.) I'd get up early, forego breakfast, and drive back into town in time for class, because I was the type of student who would rather crawl naked over hot coals than even consider missing an 8 AM class. These overnighters were not exactly Himalayan expeditions, but they were a damned site better than staying at home watching *M*A*S*H** re-runs and doing bong hits with my roommates, Fekete the Schitzo and his loyal sidekick, Blind Lloyd.

These days, it seems like it takes me three days to plan a weekend backpacking trip. Spontaneity is no longer part of my personal outdoors equation. Now, admittedly, living in a land dominated by severe winter has something to do—for at least half the year—with that reality, but far less than I would have myself believe.

I've sort of got myself caught up in a very ironic High Country mentality. Despite our location, this is not a camping-oriented community. Oh, sure, just about everyone hereabouts owns camping/backpacking gear, and just about everyone uses that gear several times a year. But, for the most part, the people who live here utilize the backcountry predominantly for two- or three-hour exercise-oriented excursions. And I, too, have taken up that habit.

And I have determined to break that habit. I have always felt uncomfortable with the "wilderness-as-workout-facility" perspective that pervades the High Country. Yet, I have become about as wrapped up in that perspective as anyone can be. I no longer think in terms of "going for a walk in the woods." These days, whether I articulate it to myself or not, my forays into the backcountry are mainly for exercise. Like most people who live here, I start feeling guilty if I go more than a day without "working out." So, when I head up the North Tenmile Creek Trail, which starts a stone's throw from where I live, I do so primarily to get the heart rate going. To say I no longer stop to smell the columbines is an understatement. After all, you risk minimizing the aerobic benefit of your workout when you stop to admire the local flora.

Now, when you start thinking along these lines, you are apt to make personal comparisons with the past. Back in the days when I spent almost as much time in the woods as I did out of them, I was a serious social mutant. Maybe there is logic in that reality, because the less time you spend in civilization, the less civilized you are apt to be.

I probably interface as well with my fellow man these days as I ever have, and that could possibly be attributed to the fact that I now have the opportunity to practice more. I do not often run off for weeks on end, specifically to be by my lonesome forty-seven miles from the closest dirt road, as much as I used to.

And, while that may be well and good—beings as I have a gig that requires an ability to deal with people fairly positively fairly frequently—it still makes me feel at least a little unclean, because I really don't give a hoot in hell about interfacing well with my fellow man. I used to be perfectly happy being a member in good stead of a small circle of nasty, gnarly muchachos, and the hell with everyone else.

I miss that spontaneous, heavily outdoors-oriented M. John. And I can't help but feel that the M. John of old, the one that I miss, the one who's nickname was Jumpin' Jack Flash, has withered away and died simultaneously with his camping consciousness.

This weekend, I leave for a couple of weeks of R&R down in southwestern New Mexico—psychic "ground zero," as it were. I plan to spend zero nights indoors, unless, of course, I get arrested at the Buffalo Bar in downtown Silver City and hauled off to the slammer. I plan to sleep on the ground above the Lower Gila Box Canyon, outside Lordsburg. I plan to hike for a few days along the Black Range Divide Trail, where the view of the sunrise over the Rio Grande Valley is easy on the eye. I plan to wallow in the Turkey Creek Hot Springs for a minimum of two days, getting out only long enough to refill my beverage cup.

And maybe I'll even drive by Little Cherry Creek Campground, just to see if any ghosts of camping past are hanging out. If they are, I hope like hell they tackle me, tie me up, and hold a mirror up to my face. It would be interesting to see what I look like under those circumstances.

A Trail Runs Through Me

In the past several months, I have given even more thought than usual to the subject of long-distance hiking trails. As one who has completed both the 2,100-mile Appalachian Trail, which runs from Maine to Georgia, and the 470-mile Colorado Trail, which runs through Summit County on its way from Denver to Durango, it should not be surprising that long-distance-trail matters catch my attention.

Summit County is in the process of becoming the long-distance-trail capital of the Known Universe. In addition to having forty-some-odd miles of the Colorado Trail in our backyard, we will, in the next few years, also be home to the Continental Divide National Scenic Trail, which connects the Mexican and Canadian borders, and the American Discovery Trail, this country's first coast-to-coast footpath.

My friends and coworkers, who have to listen to me babble on and on about how cool it is to have all these miles of long-distance trails traversing the Summit, have come to (tactfully, I might add) start voicing some degree of perplexedness over my enthusiasm for this subject. Their points, and they are points well taken, center around the not-unique-to-Fayhee's-coworkers-and-friends curiosity regarding what the hell difference there is between having several hundred miles of just regular Forest Service hiking trails in your backyard and having several hundred miles of long-distance, properly named trails in your backyard.

That's a question well-asked, and one that, on a practical, day-to-day level, probably is tough to answer. If you're out riding your mountain bike on a trail, it really matters not one iota on the practical, experiential level if it's a twenty-mile segment of the Divide Trail or a twenty-mile hodgepodge of just regular ol' schmucky trails that begin and end right here in Summit County. Nonetheless, I hope people will get a little more enthusiastic about these cool things called long-distance trails that make their way on their meandering routes from somewhere else to somewhere else still.

A few months ago, I finished a fairly long story for *Backpacker* magazine titled "Radical Repeaters," wherein I interviewed, and wrote about, nine different people who were not just addicted to long-distance hiking, but were pretty much addicted to one or two trails in particular, the Appalachian Trail being the main one. In preparing that story, I talked with one person who had hiked the Appalachian Trail ten times. I talked with one guy who had flip-flopped the AT twice—meaning he hiked the trail end-to-end, turned around and hiked it again, then turned around and hiked it yet again. I talked with one guy who hiked the AT, the Continental Divide Trail, and the Pacific Crest Trail over the course of three consecutive summers. I talked with another who had hiked 16,000 miles in the past five years, all of it on long-distance trails.

The first thing to understand about those people is that, from top to bottom, soup to nuts, they all seemed borderline nuts. Not dangerous nuts or anything. Just a little out-of-kilter. Yet, like most nuts, they had some valuable observations, about life, about long-distance backpacking, and about long-distance trails.

If I could distill nine fairly disparate perspectives into one observation about long-distance trails, it would come out as the "beauty of connectedness."

Over the fifty-some-odd-year development of both the AT and the Pacific Crest Trail, people from many parts of the country came together to make those trails happen and, in so doing, they presented not only wonderful opportunities for personal adventure, but for connections to be made between the people and places along those trails.

This point is especially poignant along the AT, where sister city relationships have developed between trail towns, and where, if you hail from, say, Hanover, New Hampshire, then you share something mighty important with the good folks down in Damascus, Virginia. And that would be the AT, which passes through the middle of both towns.

One of the observations I make to non-Rocky Mountain dwellers about the culture of the Mountain Time Zone is that people who dwell in these parts do not think in terms of regionality one bit. We in the Colorado High Country understand, of course, that we have this thing called the "Rockies" in common with people in New Mexico and Montana, yet we do not think that we have anything in common culturally.

Historically, the people of northern Georgia have no more, and no less, in common with the people of northwest New Jersey than we do with our mountain-dwelling brethren in Wyoming. But, when the AT was completed, there was, all of a sudden, an umbilical cord of commonality that has led to much in the way of cultural interaction between the communities of northern Georgia and northwest New Jersey. And that, I believe, is a good thing—a good thing that is caused by something as simple as a hiking trail.

Another thing I gleaned from my "Radical Repeaters" interviews was that having long-distance trails in one's neighborhood breeds curiosity and adventuresomeness in local populations—both positive attributes. Kids who know there's an ADT passing a few miles from their front porch naturally grow curious about where that trail leads. They learn that one three-foot-wide ribbon of dirt goes to someplace called "Kentucky" and to another place called "Nevada"—places they probably wouldn't give two thoughts to otherwise.

Just about every one of the Radical Repeaters I talked with, and an extremely high percentage of the people I met while hiking the Appalachian Trail, grew up near the AT. They dayhiked on it as children. And they grew up dreaming about hiking the whole thing, from end-to-end, someday. Those kinds of dreams are good kinds of dreams, dreams based on a notion of adventure and experience and seeing new places and meeting new people.

I have never had much interest in visiting Europe. Well, actually, I wouldn't mind visiting Europe, it's just that there's so many damned Europeans over there. But, if you can make judgments about a place you've never visited, I would say that one of the coolest things about Europe is that you can literally walk all over the entire continent on marked, established long-distance trails.

With the CDNST, the ADT, the AT, the PCT, the North Country Trail, and the Pacific Northwest Trail, we are getting to the point as a country where a person could just strike out and explore a high percentage of this great nation—on foot.

I was talking the other day to Jim Wolf, the founder and president of the Continental Divide Trail Society, headquartered in Metro D.C. We were, of course, talking about the CDNST, and one of the biggest disappointments he expressed to me was the fact that the residents of the Rockies have not embraced that trail, even though, when completed, it will run through the heart of our home turf.

When he asked me why I thought the CDNST was not more popularly supported, in terms of advocacy, cash, and time, I responded that, by and large, people here have not yet learned to love long-distance hiking trails to the degree that they will volunteer time, money, and sweat to establish them. I also told him that maybe one day they—we—would.

After all, we're sitting at the crossroads.

Fond and Not-so-Fond Memories of Monkey Wrenching

I have always been of the opinion that nostalgia, in most of its permutations and gradations, is a not-so-positive thing, an attitude especially unbecoming in the leave-your-old-life-behind-you-oriented West. There are, however, justifiable exceptions to this attitude—especially if the thing(s) you are nostalgia-izing about happen to have happened after you already left your old life behind and moved to the leave-your-old-life-behind-you-oriented West.

And those exceptions invariably drop into one's Here & Now via hopelessly external forces. There you are walking down the street with your hands in your pockets and an otherwise innocent song on your lips when, POW!, a reason to ponder your past and the part your past plays in your present smacks your otherwise content self right upside the head. Such has been the case for me over the course of the now-infamous South Barton Gulch Timber Sale controversy. More specifically, the threat by an anonymous letter to the editor writer that the timber sale had been spiked brought back some memories, ones that had been happily stashed away—partially because of wisdom gained from age and partially because I now have a wife who puts up with very little in the way of tomfoolery on the part of her husband—in psyche-land.

In days now buried so deep in the recesses of my mainframe that they scarcely seem part of my current life, I was, using a tennis rating system, about a 3.5-rated practitioner of ecotage. (Concurrently, I was a 5.0- to 5.5-rated tennis player, if that's worth anything.) I was living in a part of the country where the concept of doing things like spiking trees, chain sawing billboards, and modifying the mechanical processes of front-end loaders was conceived and born. If not exactly commonplace, these endeavors, known generically as "monkey wrenching," after the late Edward Abbey's novel *The Monkey Wrench Gang*, were not entirely unheard of. To say the least.

That the notion of monkey wrenching was popular in the part of the country in which I then dwelled was not, is not, and should not be surprising. Abbey lived about two hours away from where I lived. The radical environmental group, Earth First!, which popularized monkey wrenching, was "formed" on the land next door to one of my buddies, a sometimes roommate.

My college buddies and I were in no way, shape, or form at the cutting edge of the monkey wrenching consciousness, even though many of the people we associated with were. People we drank beer with were people who actually came up with the philosophical and practical rationales for participating in ecotage. We rapturously listened to them, read the appropriate "educational" material in the now-defunct *Earth First! Journal* and, at least ten or twelve times, set out into the hot desert night armed with ample amounts of carbonated beverages and proceeded, for predominantly recreational purposes you understand, to wreak as much havoc as possible upon whatever symptom of "progress" it was that happened to catch our collective eye that particular weekend.

And, I must confess, these forays into the land of the easily convictable felony(ies) were about as fun as fun can get with your clothes on. For, though I do not now, in retrospect, attach as much in the way of deep thought to our actions as I would like, at the time, we actually, on some primitive level, thought we were doing some "good." Now, mind you, none of us thought we were really contributing to a strategy that would ultimately alter anything of significance. I mean, we did not believe, on any level, that cutting down a billboard advertising a condominium complex we happened to oppose because it would blight the view from one of our favorite mesa tops would actually make the condominium-builders realize the errors of their ways, tossing the tools of their destructive trade into some arroyo before becoming card-carrying members of Greenpeace.

Far from it. We just thought that it would be shitloads of fun to assume the role of burrs-under-the-development-saddle. And, for a half-dozen mostly drunk college students in an inconsequential part of an inconsequential state, that was damned well good enough.

Then, by God, one day something *serious* happened on the monkey wrenching front right under our noses, and it basically scared the living piss out of us. I and a couple of amigos, several of whom are amigos still, were "exploring" the possibility to "repairing" a few pieces of seismic testing equipment just outside one of our favorite local wilderness areas. Some Texas oil company was considering looking for oil and gas in the Aldo Leopold Wilderness. While we were still several miles from the place where we intended to repair the aforesaid equipment, we all saw a stream of the blackest of black smoke billowing into the sky. Something smelled fishy, and we retired to our vehicles for a rapid return trip home.

Come to find out that some good-hearted soul had taken this potential oil and gas exploration stuff to heart to a degree that our teensy little cojones could not have imagined. Seems "person or persons unknown" (no arrests were ever made, to the best of my knowledge) had the same basic idea as we did. But, rather than adjusting a few screws here and there on seismic testing equipment, which we probably wouldn't have recognized if it walked up and bit us on the butt, the person or persons unknown had walked up to an unmanned oil-company-owned helicopter (the pilot, come to find out, was back in the woods making number two), dumped several gallons of some flammable fluid onto it, and tossed an incendiary device into the cockpit.

Boom.

That was the smoke we saw.

I've always chuckled heartily at the thought of that poor schmuck pilot walking out of the woods, feeling mighty good and relieved, right up until the point where he notices that a million-dollar helicopter, which he is responsible for, has just exploded. (I knew all these details, by the way, because I was working for a local newspaper at the time, and actually had to write a few stories on this incident, all the while acting innocent like, which, when you get right down to it, I was.)

Of course, it's one thing to chain saw a couple of billboards, and it's one thing to get caught chain sawing a couple of billboards (something I, fortunately, never experienced). It's quite another thing to know that, on the only dirt road into a place where a helicopter owned by a huge oil company was just toasted, there were tire tracks bearing a striking resemblance to my van's tire tracks.

For weeks and weeks, even as I was writing stories about "how the investigation was continuing" into the helicopter torching (I couldn't believe how serious the cops were about this case), I was sitting around getting plowed with my cohorts-in-would-be crime with puckered sphincters waiting for a pounding on the door harkening arrest warrants stemming not from what we were planning on doing (hell, we would never have torched a helicopter; tried to fly it away, maybe, but never torched it) but, rather, from the fact that we were in the vicinity with admittedly decidedly nefarious intentions, coincidentally at the same time something fairly captivating in the criminal sense was transpiring.

In short, right then and there, I retired post haste from the monkey wrenching game, nevermore to become unretired. I need to point out, though, that, perhaps by coincidence, and perhaps not, all oil and gas exploration drilling outside that particular wilderness area stopped cold the day that helicopter was torched.

I must admit, though, that I felt a little bit of the old rush when I read that anonymous letter stating that trees in South Barton Gulch had been spiked. I thought that, maybe just maybe, some of the old fire was still alive in the world. And, I must admit that I felt more than a little bit sad when no spikes were found. Sure, it takes chutzpah just to make a threat. But, to steal a line from a TV commercial, chutzpah don't feed the bulldog. The South Barton Gulch Timber Sale has gone through. And the trees in question are there no more.

If a Tree Falls in the Forest . . .

There was a time and place in my journalistic life when and where, if you would have told me that I would be writing a book chapter even slightly in defense of the U.S. Forest Service (which, in a way, is exactly what this is), I would have asked you to please share whatever hallucinogens you were on with me.

This attitude is easily explainable. When I was in the process of cutting my journalistic teeth and, concurrently, honing my intense professional dislike and distrust of any and all things and people even remotely federal-government-related, I happened to be living in southwestern New Mexico, very near the Gila National Forest. The Gila is the largest contiguous national forest in the lower forty-eight states. It is home to the 500,000-acre Gila Wilderness, the world's first legally designated wilderness area. It was the home turf for Geronimo, Mangus Colorado, and, for a while, Aldo Leopold. It is a mighty special place in many ways. It is also home base for the most-backwards-assed redneck mentality this side of Pig Squeal, West Virginia.

The notion thereabouts was, and to a certain extent still is, that the Gila National Forest existed/exists solely for the purpose of providing grist for the mills of the extractive industries. Cattle grazing, mining, and timbering were and are held in a degree of esteem in that part of the country that is without equal in Colorado, even in the far west of the Western Slope. Consequently, the Gila National Forest supervisor's office, located in Silver City, where I lived for five years, has always been phenomenally adept at kowtowing to the every beck and whim of the extractive industries. In the Gila, there have been many, many examples of egregious behavior on the part of the Forest Service in its attempts to give the extractive industries whatever they want, whenever they want it. The Endangered Species Act has been kicked in the gonads. The Wilderness Act has been sidestepped. The Environmental Impact Statement process, as outlined in the National Environmental Policy Act, has been expectorated upon.

It is tempting to compare the power of the extractive industries vis-à-vis influence on the Forest Service in southwestern New Mexico with the power the ski areas boast hereabouts. But, that comparison would do the reality of the situation very little justice because the extractive industries in that part of the country are far, far more powerful in a relative sense.

Anyhow, because I have always maintained a rather well-developed anti-extractive-industries attitude, I came to distrust the Forest Service to a degree that transcended the Gila National Forest powers that be. This was the attitude towards the Forest Service I brought with me to Colorado when I moved here in 1984 and, by and large, it is my attitude still.

Yet, even understanding all that, I find myself mentally rising in defense of my local manifestation of the Forest Service: the Dillon Ranger District (DRD) of the Arapaho National Forest. And, the specific context that causes this mental defense is the many manifestations of this beast called "timbering."

Now, I want to stress two things. First, 99.9 percent of the time, I am against any and all variations on the timbering theme. As anyone with even a molecule of gray matter knows full well, when it comes to commercial timbering operations, the Forest Service has not, uh, traditionally been praised by the environmental community.

Next, it needs to be known that I have not exactly become a pro-Forest Service crusader. The agency's sordid extraction-based past makes any and all components of the Forest Service very worthy of constant (and intense) public and media scrutiny. That said, I'm getting mighty sick and tired of the way the DRD is being perceived and treated these days when it comes to timbering operations hereabouts.

Of all the natural world abuses the Forest Service is guilty of, timbering is perhaps the most palpable. Even though much ado has been made of the Forest Service's recent decisions to cut board-feet extraction in half nationally and to eliminate below-cost timber sales entirely, completely unjustifiable timbering abuses are still continuing on a massive scale in many parts of the country, especially the Pacific Northwest. The economic power of the timber industry in those parts makes it all but impossible for the Forest Service to even pretend that it has progressed in an enlightenment sense far from the dark ages of "multiple use."

Such is not the case here in Summit County. Commercial timbering interests have certainly walked hand-in-hand through Summit County's woods with the DRD in the very recent past. Even though, given half a chance and another change in political climate, I know full well that such a relationship could easily be renewed with companies like Louisiana-Pacific, by and large I believe DRD District Ranger Jeff Bailey when he says that the days of large, commercial timber cuts in Summit County are largely behind us, unless you count the clearing of ski runs as clear cuts, which you should.

Anyhow, even though Bailey has said time and time again that timber cuts are essentially a part of the DRD's deep, dark past, we find ourselves frequently reading in the local papers that more timber cuts are being planned and executed in Summit County. And, this is where I'm starting to get a little peeved, as well as perplexed.

I have spent a lot of time in the woods here, in other states, and abroad with professional "foresters"—a title that is justifiably being retooled because of its tree-cutting, "timber management" connotations. I have come to look at the vast majority of professional foresters as people to be closely watched, mainly because the vast majority of them have been educated and indoctrinated by a system that looks at the trees of our national forests as potentially exploitable commodities, rather than critical components of ecosystems.

But, that said and understood, I have also come to grudgingly realize that professional foresters know a lot more about the way fragmented, non-ecosystem-intact forests function than, as a random example, me. Even if the Forest Service's timber-related knowledge is referenced by a desire to allow commercial timber cuts for no other reason than economics, it is still more ecological knowledge than I, or any other writer I know hereabouts, have about the way forests work and, more importantly in this context, don't work.

I am well aware that the DRD has made a lot of boneheaded decisions, on the political as well as ecological fronts, in Summit County when it comes to the cutting of trees. Bailey has contended to me on several occasions that serious errors in judgment like the South Barton and Wise Mountain timber harvests were (1) made years ago, and (2) conceptually things of the past. Of course, as much as I like Bailey as a person, it must be remembered, when he makes statements like that, that he is, first and foremost, a member in good stead of the U.S. federal bureaucracy and, therefore, his statements must be taken with a grain of salt, especially when you consider that there is at least one more substantial clear cut, Spring Creek, slated to take place sometime in the next few years on DRD territory.

Bailey argues that the Forest Service is obligated to honor timber contracts it made before it became the enlightened, ecologically oriented agency it claims to be today. That may or may not be true (Tim Glasco of the Blue River Group of the Sierra Club claims it is definitely not true). Anyhow, here and now, the proposed Spring Creek Timber Sale is an aside. As it gets closer to the time when the chain saws get fired up, the public will make its opinions known to Bailey and the DRD about that particular timber sale. What is not an aside here and now are the other timber management projects scheduled for DRD lands. For instance, there has been much public uproar recently admonishing the DRD to nix its plans to cut some trees near Miner's Creek. Also, the DRD has given tours of areas near Straight Creek and Sapphire Point to show interested parties what they want to do, timber management-wise, in those areas.

The argument against the timber management project near Miner's Creek is especially ironic. The crux of the anti-cutting story is that Miner's Creek is a very popular area with tourists and residents alike and, therefore, ought to be spared the chain saw. The argument further states that, since Summit County is so tourist-dependent, and since tourists come here to see trees, not clear cuts, we ought to leave the trees be, lest the tourists leave Summit County be.

This argument is no more valid than a logger's argument in Washington State that his job will go down the toilet if timber harvests are diminished in the name of spotted owl habitat protection. It is, and will always be, my argument that economics, whether based on tourism or logging, should not play an active role in the way the Forest Service goes about making its land management decisions. Those decisions ought to be made solely on the basis of ecological necessity. And, anyone who does not believe there is significant ecological necessity to cut trees in Summit County has his/her head in the sand.

I say again: the forests here are pitifully unhealthy. We have monogrowth forests of similar age and that (1) is not the way Mother Nature intended it, and (2) is getting dangerous. I recently talked with one firefighter-type friend of mine who contends, in no uncertain terms, that Summit County is ripe for a one-hundred-year, Yellowstone-like fire. The sad state of our forests is the main culprit in that regard.

You think tourists don't want to see clear cuts, just wait until they are faced with scorched hillsides, à la Yellowstone in 1988. There are two main points here. First, I'm not saying that we should leave the DRD to is own devices. Quite the contrary. The Forest Service should be watched and scrutinized in all regards, including, but certainly not limited to, timbering operations. The agency's poor past track record justifies intense public scrutiny.

Next, the people in this county are getting ready to face a DRD-related set of choices, and those choices will, on the surface, seem mighty distasteful. But, in a sense, the recent tree-thinning proposals serve as an introduction to those choices, for the public, as well as for the Forest Service.

Sometime in the near future, the DRD will embark on a countywide ecosystem planning process. This process will be much like the recent Dillon Reservoir Ecosystem Management Plan, though it will be of a much greater scale. The idea is that Summit County's forests are a far cry from what they would be if European culture had never made the scene. (The Utes had very few world-class ski resorts.) No one is saying that we ought to try to restore our local forests to their pre-1800 form, because, of course, such an undertaking would be impossible. But Bailey and his clan would like to see the area's biodiversity restored as much as possible, given modern land-use constraints. And, such a restoration project will involve cutting the hell out of a lot of trees in Summit County.

I'm not arguing that we should simply get used to tree cutting, because a lot more is going to follow. What I am saying is, let's stop screeching every time a tree is felled by the people who know more about trees than any of us. Our forests need trees to be felled. Not always. Not in all places. But many times, in many places.

Now a lot of people are going to start sweating about the thought of whole hillsides of lodgepoles being cut in order to make room for, say, spruces—even though those people may believe, on a visceral level, that increasing the area's biodiversity is a good thing. Those people are going to start worrying that tourists will want to visit other places, for aesthetic reasons.

Perhaps so, but, hell, we can live with a few less tourists. We might even come to like living with a few less tourists. More than that, though, the county's marketing machinery, which sometimes is astute, and sometimes isn't, could, without working too hard, turn such a grandiose forest management consciousness to its favor or, failing that, at least embark on a program of damage control that shouldn't take a genius to pull off.

When tourists want to know what's going on with Summit County's forests, once the ecosystem management plan kicks in, just boastfully tell them the truth, which amounts to this: we live in an enlightened place, a place that's together enough that we are willing to sacrifice a little in the way of visual aesthetics here and there, and maybe even a little in the way of prosperity in order to help our local ecosystem regain its health and well-being. There is, for example, ample opportunity for interpretive tours of this proposed ecosystem restoration project, just like the Park Service has been doing in Yellowstone since the fires.

Of course, we all need to keep our eyes on the DRD, just in case they end up using the idea of ecosystem restoration as a modern-day excuse to lay a little wood on Louisiana-Pacific. (And, if that's what ends up happening, Bailey ought to be tarred and feathered and run out of town.) In the meantime, when it comes to timber management programs being instigated in the name of forest health in Summit County, let's not let the trees obscure our vision of the woods.

With Noses Pointed Upwards

In early January 1994, my wife, Gay, and I attended the opening gala of that season's Keystone Science School Mountain Speaker Series. The event kicked off with an hour's worth of silent auctioning, cocktailing, and hobnobbing, which is about as pleasant a way to spend sixty minutes as I can think of.

The evening's entertainment was provided by a man named Dick Bass, who is the owner/founder of Utah's Snowbird Ski Resort and author of the book *Seven Summits.* Bass was scheduled to talk about the quest that served as the meat of the story for *Seven Summits.* That quest consisted of a successful multi-year effort to become the first man to climb the highest peaks on each of the seven continents.

Gay and I attended Bass's talk despite the fact that it was going to center on the topic of mountain climbing. Though we are devotees of the Mountain Speaker Series (I, myself, have participated in it twice), neither Gay nor I are really attracted to slide show presentations by mountain climbers. In the past couple of years, we've attended Mountain Speaker Series talks by the likes of John Roskelley and Jeff Lowe, both of whom are world-class climbers. We enjoyed those talks well enough, but mainly because John and Jeff are such nice hombres, as well as being at least moderately entertaining.

But, by and large, mountain climbers, by definition, do not have a lot in common with non-mountain climbers, and that reality becomes very palpable when the vast majority of them make public presentations. By and large, whenever an expedition-type mountain climber makes a public presentation, the audience becomes instantly divided into climber and non-climber camps. And the bulk of presentations by climbers are appealing only to members of the former which, in a way, makes perfect sense but, in another way, is rude as hell.

Anyhow, imagine our surprise when we enjoyed Bass's presentation about as much as we have ever enjoyed listening to a public speaker in our lives. Even though Bass managed to drag his butt to the summits of Denali, Aconcagua, Everest, Vinson Massif, Kilimanjaro, Kosciusko, and Elbrus, he is not a mountain climber per se, much less a climber cut from the classic mold.

Boy, we were relieved. Bass managed to recount his climbing experiences, and the life stories that led up to those experiences, in such a way that your average person in the audience reacted like, "Hey, that's exactly how *I* would feel under similar circumstances." There was no bravado, false or otherwise, except for the bravado that justifiably comes hand-in-hand with having climbed peaks like Denali and Everest without dying in the process. Neither was there any of the sickening understated humor for which climbers are so well known. "And here's a shot of me hanging by one fingernail from the top of a 5,000-foot cliff. It was steep. I was getting hungry and, boy, was it ever windy."

Anyhow, despite the fact that Bass invoked the name of God about a billion times during his talk (something I do not personally like but which, coming out of his Texas-drawl-dominated mouth, seemed contextual), I found myself telling people all over the county the next day what a great speaker Bass was. Then I found myself being confronted by as much in the way of vehement, vicious, venomous disagreement as I have found myself facing in a very long time. It was as though, by not actively condemning Bass as a person as well as a climber, I was being judged guilty by association by a lot of people I would have thought were incapable of such judgments. One person I talked to described Bass as the "man who bought his way up Everest." Another told me that he wouldn't accept a copy of *Seven Summits* if it was offered to him for free.

Now, I can understand that there might have been people who did not like Bass's Mountain Speaker Series presentation because they did not like the way he told stories. He spoke quickly and, often, seemingly disjointedly. But, he managed to intertwine anecdotes with philosophy with personal history with poetry in such an expert manner that his journeys down "tangent lane" were, in my opinion, easily forgivable. As well, I could see where people would have been disappointed in Bass's slides. He took most of them himself, and he is no professional picture-taker. At the same time, the only camera he carried with him during his Seven Summit quests was an Olympus-XA, so his lack of ability as a photographer was not mitigated in the least by a wide array of the latest in camera technology.

The negative feedback I was getting transcended all that. It centered not on style but, rather, of the fact that Bass was obviously not a member in good stead of the community of climbers. He had simply decided one day that he was going to try to reach the summit of the highest mountains on each of the continents, and he basically hired professional mountaineers to help him achieve that goal. Not exactly the dues-paying process that most mountain climbers have to go through before they summit Everest, but—so what? Bass said right up front during his talk that, without the help of the "real" mountaineers he hired, he would never have made it to the tops of at least four of those seven summits.

Anyhow, the acrimony I heard expressed about Bass led me to read *Seven Summits.* The book itself is no more than okay. Bass hired Rick Ridgeway, another world-class mountaineer and a decent enough writer, to actually pen the work. It was obvious from the first word on that the author was hired to write *Seven Summits.* It came across as much like a long press release as it did a creative work of nonfiction.

The book really didn't shed any additional light on Bass. What I saw and heard at the Mountain Speaker Series was essentially what I read in *Seven Summits.* What the book did do was shed a little light on the mountaineering community, which apparently considers Bass to be a creature more suited to four legs than two.

It is easy to understand why people would have trouble with Bass's personality. He is obviously the butt-hole, affluent Texan we all love to hate. He does, indeed, come across like someone who feels there is no problem on earth—including his quest to bag the Seven Summits—that cannot be solved with a huge infusion of cash. And, as anyone who has paid any attention whatsoever to the world of mountain climbing at all can attest, a dearth of cash pretty much sums up that world. There are literally hundreds of climbers out there capable, with a little luck, of making it to the top of the Seven Summits, were it not for the minuscule problem of a lack of money.

It took Bass four attempts at Everest before he summited. And he bankrolled every one of those expeditions—at a cost of more than $250,000 per expedition. He was twice added to climbing rosters solely because of his fiscal contributions to those expeditions. His Antarctica foray was even more expensive—almost $1 million. Again, he bankrolled that trip.

So, I suppose the main problem the climbing community has with Bass is a sort of reverse arrogance, a snobbishness that is generally stereotypically associated as coming from people like Bass, rather than towards him. (It is ironic to note that, because of Bass's dollars, many climbers who could never have afforded to climb Everest, Denali, Vinson, and Aconcagua were given the opportunity to do just that.)

This elbow-rubbing with Bass and his book has brought into focus something that many people have long felt about the mountain climbing community. I once had a talk with one of the editors at *Backpacker* about what I perceived was an over-emphasis on mountaineering articles in that magazine. He, being an expedition-type climber himself, retorted that mountaineering was the highest form of backpacking and, thus, was worthy of disproportionate coverage in *Backpacker*. I disagreed, saying that, if there was such a thing as the highest form of backpacking, I felt long-distance hiking was it.

His statement punctuated the snobbishness that seems to dominate the mountaineering world, even though the stereotype of most individual climbers is one of down-to-earthiness. This snobbishness transcends the fact that mountaineering is one of the most dangerous "recreational" pursuits on earth. After all, deep-sea sailing is also extremely dangerous, and deep-sea sailors seem, jointly and severally, fairly normal, their noses generally being pointed forward, on an even keel, rather than upward, towards some self-congratulatory summit.

Now, I should point out that this undeniable snobbishness on the part of the mountaineering community does not necessarily manifest itself in day-to-day conversation with mere mortals. It does, however, manifest itself within the mountaineering community. Anyone who doubts this ought to spend a little time reading the letters to the editor sections in any of the climbing magazines. A more nit-picking, bickering, back-stabbing, whiny segment of our population would be hard to find, much less define.

And the backbone of that observation stems from the nebulous subject of mountaineering "ethics." A lot of the problems mountaineers seem to have with Bass stem from the fact that he has somehow not lived up to even the most foundational of mountaineering ethics. I think that every sport of substance, of which mountaineering is certainly one, ought to have a strong set of ethics. I don't know much about mountaineering ethics specifically, but my guess would be that Bass, as a result of his Seven Summits quest, has not recently been inducted into the Mountaineering Ethical Hall of Fame.

But, again—so freaking what? He made it to the top of the highest peak on every continent. He did what he set out to do, and he brought along a lot of people for the ride. And a decent enough yarn came out of it. All that might make many mountaineers and wannabe mountaineers see red but, from a purely non-mountaineering view, I think it's wonderful that the Keystone Science School would open its Mountain Speaker Series with someone who breaks the mountaineering mold. Which is a mentality that, seemingly, the mountaineering community itself could take to heart.

The Simple Joy of Ice-skating

In the deepest recesses of a memory that admittedly is not getting better, only richer, with age, lies the monster public ice-skating rink at Plattsburgh Air Force Base, New York, on the windy and frigid shores of Lake Champlain, high in the North Woods, much closer to Montreal than any sizable American city.

My mom decided, when I was four, that, since people in that particular part of the country generally popped out of the womb wearing freshly sharpened blades, it was high time that her eldest child—me—learned to skate, lest I lose some sort of social standing before I was even old enough to lament the thought of being a social pariah. There were no lessons planned. There was only the process of borrowing a pair of hand-me-way-way-down skates from some neighbor that would plus-or-minus fit my young feet, then driving the mile or so to the rink, then putting the skates on my feet as I sat on a snow bank, then me sitting there wondering what was going to happen next, though, at least in theory, I knew full well.

It was only the summer before that my mom had decided it was high time I learned to swim. We walked to the end of a Lake Champlain dock, she and I together, and she placed her hands under my arm pits, picked me up, my feet fluttering, and dropped my butt in no uncertain terms into the drink. Within a nanosecond, she, being a very strong swimmer, was in the water with me. And we didn't leave the water until I could keep my carcass from going blub-blub-blub down to the bottom of that huge lake, the very lake that, five years later, took the life of my stepfather.

There on the side of the rink, I knew I was in for the same kind of experience, though not exactly, because my mom was never very comfortable on ice. Once I was all laced up, she flagged down a passing skater. It was some man neither of us knew. She asked if he would take my hand and cruise me around the rink. I remember that he smiled and said he would. He towered over me. He bent down and asked if I was ready. I said I was, though I knew it didn't really matter how I answered. The plan was laid, and I was just part of the plan. The next instant, I was in the midst of the biggest G-force vortex any four-year-old could possibly imagine. My body was parallel to the rink. I was an ice skate-adorned windsock attached to the man's hand. Only occasionally did my skates even touch the ice.

It was wonderful.

My mom told me years later, as we talked about this experience for the first and only time, that that man skated me around for about half an hour. She also told me, by the time he took his leave, I was able to propel myself around the rink with typical four-year-old out-of-control abandon. She said I pretty much "took to" ice-skating. And, though, by skating standards, I have never been very good, I still harbor the ability of someone who, at an age so tender it doesn't even seem part of this increasingly decrepit adult life, took to something, something he loved and still loves and will always love.

For reasons I have never been able to figure out, ice-skating is so far down the recreational ladder in recreation-crazed Colorado that it scarcely registers. My wife, a lifelong Colorado resident, a long-time High Country dweller, and a fairly enthusiastic outdoorsperson, has ice-skated exactly once, at Keystone Resort a few years back. I am happy to report that she, too, seemed to take to the sport; she only fell once. The one night my wife skated was the one and only night I skated in my first three years in Summit County. With every change-of-the-seasons, I make vows to myself regarding what the upcoming next few months will be like for me. When the aspens started turning a few Septembers ago, I told myself this would be a winter of ice-skating.

My first three winters in Summit County, I was skateless—meaning, in order to skate, I needed to drive to Keystone or Breckenridge, the only two places in the county where one can rent skates, pay to skate, and then, finally, skate. It seemed almost as troublesome as going downhill skiing and, thus, with the exception of that one time in Keystone, I could really never be bothered.

I live in Frisco, and Frisco has its own rink. It is the kind of rink I grew up skating on. No Zamboni. No fancy facilities. No obnoxious music being played through drive-in theater speakers. Just bumpy ice with ample cracks and the kind of recreational informality that is becoming increasingly rare in the High Country. At least in this part of the High Country.

You cannot rent skates at the Frisco rink, so, during a November trip to Denver, I decided, no matter the cost, I was going to score a pair of skates.

It had been fourteen years since I last bought skates. In 1979–80, I was living in Vermont's Sugarbush (nee Mad River) Valley, and the property I lived on boasted a small pond. That winter marked my return to Winter Country. We had left Plattsburgh for the South when I was twelve. In the meantime, I had lived in Kentucky, Virginia and, much later, southwestern New Mexico—not exactly prime ice-skating states. Until I moved to Vermont, ice-skating had long ago lost its place as an active part of my existence, and I sorely lamented that reality.

And here I was in Vermont, living on a farm with a skating pond! Throughout the fall, my stomach fluttered at the thought of reacquainting myself with ice. Before winter, I stopped at a garage sale for no particular reason, and there they were: a scuffed-up pair of black figure skates that were more-or-less my size. Three bucks.

Ended up being three bucks very well spent. I figure I skated upwards of one hundred times that winter. I worked as a waiter in an Italian restaurant at the base of the ski mountain, and at the end of the work day, usually about 11 PM; I would come home, tired but hyper, and I would trudge through the knee-deep snow about a quarter mile to the pond. Often, I had to shovel the pond before I could start skating. Once that was done, I would skate hard for at least thirty minutes; sometimes, as long as an hour. That was a cold winter, and I would always return to the little farmhouse where I lived with two buddies I met the prior summer while we were all hiking the Appalachian Trail with my mustache hairs only slightly more frozen than my nose hairs and my face red and oftentimes raw. And I would sleep wonderfully. It got to the point where I had trouble sleeping if I didn't skate before retiring. A decent enough sort of addiction.

Only once that winter did I skate during daylight hours. Not once that winter did I ever share the ice with anyone else. I came to think of skating as a solitary, nocturnal habit. Like, everyone should have their own private rink, and it should be closed until dusk. And that is the way I still feel now.

I arrived in Summit County in 1989 with that same pair of $3 skates. I used them the one time I skated at Keystone with my wife. Though I understand I have little room to talk, I have to say they had not aged well. Like their owner, they were badly warped and, after only a few minutes on the ice, my feet became intolerably sore. I threw those skates away without ever using them again and became a skate-less person living in a land of ice, a place with more skating rinks than ski resorts or Nordic centers.

My wife was with me when we hit the Gart Brothers sporting goods store in the Aurora Mall. It was one of those horrible post-Thanksgiving, pre-Christmas "shopping days," when every single person alive on the planet is out and about, credit cards in-hand, looking frazzled and miserable, shopping, hating life—the kind of day that seems mighty incongruous with the messages left by the man whose birthday we are supposed to be celebrating that time of year.

We took one step into the mall, and I almost retreated in horror. Only my desire for skates pushed me through the sea of moping, holiday de-spirited humanity. The Gart Brothers store was, of course, on the opposite side of the mall from where we parked. When we finally got there, I was drenched with sweat, and I reeked of stale suburban mall stink. The skates were in the far back end of the crowded store. There were only two pairs of men's skates left. One size six. And one size ten. The latter being my size exactly.

They were hockey skates, a type I had never before used. Even though I spent my first twelve years in the Adirondacks, I never once played hockey. The game just never appealed to me, the same way soccer has never appealed to me. But, I had decided before the fact to buy a pair of hockey skates. I had no plans to take up hockey at the tender young age of thirty-five or anything; I just think hockey skates look cooler than figure skates. They cost $54, which was about half of what I expected to pay. Karma was with me all the way on this one.

I brought the new skates back to Summit County with the same air of expectation I would have had if we just bought a new puppy. The next night, I threw the skates over my shoulder and headed out into the late fall cold. The rink was deserted and had the look of ice that is most often void of other skaters, at least this time of night.

It took me a hundred years to lace the skates. Hockey skates differ significantly from figure skates in this regard: there are no D-rings. Just stiff, stubborn leather, minuscule eyelets, and laces a mile long.

Skating has been compared to riding a bike and swimming, insofar as, once you know how to do it, you never completely forget. This is, in my experience, an accurate comparison. By and large, anyone who has even slightly mastered skating knows that the operative skill is balance. Strength certainly plays its part but, in order to avoid becoming one with the ice, you have to understand and execute a very sport-specific kind of balance.

ice-skating balance is much harder to achieve than, say, Nordic skiing balance, which should not be surprising, as you are trying to stay atop two small, thin blades, rather than on two long, decidedly fatter skis. And the ramifications of falling on ice are captivating on both the intellectual and physiological levels. Admittedly, unlike downhill skiing, another sport where falling has a palpable downside, you do not have to deal with the consequences of significant momentum when you make contact with terra firma. But, unlike downhill skiing, when you fall, you, 100 percent of the time, have to deal with the consequences of your body smacking into something that's not even remotely soft. I know there is hard snow, but there is also soft snow. There is no such a thing as soft ice.

I have heard skating neophytes lament about the soreness of their ankles when they leave the rink. This is symptomatic of poor balance, nothing more. I don't really know if proper ice-skating balance can be learned in adulthood. Maybe it's like a New Yorker learning to drive a car at age twenty-six, a situation not conducive to mastery of a given activity for no other reason than the person waited too long to try to learn it. In some activities, old dogs are at a decided disadvantage.

As I first hit the ice at the Frisco rink, I remembered that I had skated a few times while living in the South. I hadn't thought about it in years. I was in about the eighth grade and, during one of those winters that old timers still talk about, a small section of Beaver Dam Swamp, behind my buddy Gerry Wass's house, froze up. The local kid population, completely unused to being able to dial into any form of pure winter recreation, poured onto the ice, wide-eyed and mystified. Old mildew-filled pairs of skates began appearing from musty boxes in the attics of ancient Colonial houses. There were six-year-olds wearing size twelve white lady's figure skates and high schoolers wearing double-blades clipped onto penny loafers. We were not going to be confused with people from northern Minnesota.

We decided that we were going to play hockey. Only problem was, we were a little short on hockey gear. Everyone went home and fashioned homemade hockey sticks out of scrap lumber. Our puck was a square of two-by-four. Our hockey rink was, out of necessity, S-shaped, because we had to deal with an unfortunate tree-growing-in-the-middle-of-the-swamp problem.

We were also a little short on even a rudimentary understanding of the game. I was chosen to referee the hockey game, because I had once lived in an area where hockey was played for real. Ample qualifications in Tidewater, Virginia.

What came out of the situation was Southern Swamp Hockey. It has not caught on internationally, though it should have. I would call penalties, like "cussin' while the puck is not bein' hit," for which the punishment would be a big pile-on on the offending cusser.

Our orgy of ice-skating lasted about two days. Then the cold snap snapped, and Beaver Dam Swamp returned to its swampy ways and, to the best of my knowledge, it hasn't froze up since. At least not like that.

My first laps around the Frisco rink were, to say the least, tentative. I preferred to reacquaint myself with the ice without broken elbows. But, it wasn't long before I was skating probably as well as

I have ever skated. Ice-skating, to me, is one of those sports that stands to be ruined if one tries to improve too much. Now, of course, I'm not talking about competition figure skating or hockey or speed skating. I'm talking about just skating around the damned rink late at night by your lonesome after a few beers, sometimes clockwise, sometimes counter-clockwise and, sometimes, when you're feeling bold, diagonally across the ice. On the self-improvement front, it's okay to try to not fall too often. And it's acceptable to try to skate backwards once or twice every session, as long as you are not very successful. But, besides that, you ought to just get out there and skate. "Improvement," however you want to define that word, is certainly going to make its way into your Here & Now, despite your best efforts to the contrary, so you ought not push it too hard.

Even though ice-skating is one of my favorite pastimes, I have never, even when I was ten and amigos all around me were getting better and better every season, had a desire to do anything more than skate noncompetitively around a rink, which might strike a lot of people as extremely uninteresting, but I consider it very Zen-like. Like chopping wood, another boring activity I love.

As I said, hockey simply never appealed to me. I have always considered it kinda dull, and I never much liked the toothless aggressiveness inherent in the game. And competitive figure skating, though beautiful to watch, never attracted me, either. It always seemed a little too dilettantish for my Bohemian tastes, though the thought of holding an in-shape young lady wearing a mini-skirt up over my head by her rear-end did at one time, before I was married (*long* before I was married), seem like something I could get used to, given enough practice.

If there is one form of competitive skating that did once sort of attract me, it was speed skating. I tried it a couple of times when I was very young, but I lost interest because of the uni-directional nature of the sport. I might have gone for it more if speed-skating rinks were figure-eight-shaped or if there were on-rink obstacles, like something out of American Gladiators. But, maybe not.

No, I've always eschewed traditional ice sports, preferring to just tool around the rink at a speed that would make Henry David Thoreau wince with impatience. It's the kind of activity that frees up the brain, not that my brain is kept in chains ordinarily or anything.

Now, with regards to non-traditional ice sports, my opinion is a little different, both from the spectator and participant perspectives. About my tenth time out on the rink last winter, there were five teenagers out skating when I arrived. They were playing mayhemish ice-skating games—the kind I grew up playing, the kind I would have thought that I would not consider, for one instant, playing at my geezerish age. They were playing Ultimate Frisbee, "crack the whip" and piling on each other every twenty or so seconds for no apparent good reason, which is the best reason of all for piling on someone. When I was a kid, we would play "Red Rover," tag, and tackle football on ice. Minor injuries were many and, no matter what, someone would always end up going home in tears. It was a great way to spend Adirondack winter afternoons that were not long, but seemed long.

I spent more time that night watching those five teenagers frolicking about than I did actually skating, and this from someone who would rather punch himself in the nads that sit through five minutes of game seven of a Stanley Cup Finals. After a while, they asked if I wanted to play a little Frisbee with them. And, suddenly, there I was, jostling around on the ice with kids half my age, falling on my ass, knocking them on theirs and participating in several pile-ons. It was great, though I ached for days afterward.

My mom, who died several years ago, would have been mightily amused.

This very well might be the last year for the Frisco Ice Rink as I have come to know and appreciate and maybe even need it. Meadow Creek Park is located adjacent the "Frisco Triangle," the last major undeveloped parcel of land in town. The plan at this point is for a fairly substantial housing development to be built on the triangle's seventy-some-odd acres.

With that development, of course, will likely come many more people down here at night to savor the sweetness of the ice—especially because the Frisco town government is talking about making "improvements" here at the rink. They're talking about installing additional lighting, setting up a little skate rental shop/warming hut and building restrooms. It wouldn't surprise me if someone somewhere along the development line decided to pipe in some obnoxious music through drive-in movie speakers. And I can see a day when the town buys a Zamboni, meaning the rink's bumps, divots, and cracks will become, like many simple High Country things, a thing of the past. I'm sure there will be a fee charged to skate, and I imagine lessons will be available.

And, naturally, if all that happens, people will start having to skate in a counter-clockwise direction. There will be no packs of teenagers playing Ultimate Frisbee, because it will not be allowed. Rather, there will be rosy-cheeked couples skating arm-in-arm, scads of young people unceasingly yelling at the top of their lungs, and probably even some competent skaters executing spins and twirls and such.

There are worse scenarios, I know, and I am a crotchety old sack of crap for growling for even a moment about what most people would see as a logical and desirable evolution of a recreational amenity in one of the nation's premier resort communities.

But, hell, that's the way, and the only way, things go in the resort part of the High Country. It is the only operational mentality. I have lived here long enough to comprehend the lay of the cultural land hereabouts, and never once, once folks (especially folks involved in local government and/or some variation of the development theme—which seemingly covers about half the population) start talking about "improving" something, have I seen a decision made to leave that something alone. And I am getting sick of that mentality.

Dammit, what is it about the High Country resort consciousness that fails to comprehend the benefits and pleasures of simplicity and primitiveness? Why does everything have to be made bigger and better in the name of an improved recreational experience? I feel like I should—at gunpoint, if necessary—bring everyone who supports the notion of "improving" this rink down here on the coldest night of the winter and make them skate and skate and skate until some little light bulb goes on over their joint and several noggins, and they say, "Yeah, this is cool the way it is."

But, as we all know, you can lead government officials and developers to the ice, but you can't make them think.

No matter where you live, there are geographic-specific skills that every resident of that area ought to be familiar with. In the Colorado's

High Country, everyone ought to know how to ski, of course. And everyone ought to know how to Nordic ski, how to scream properly during a high-speed black-ice spinout, how to chop wood and start a cozy, romantic fire in the fireplace, how to change a flat tire during a raging blizzard on Hoosier Pass at 2:30 AM after spending six straight hours holding up the bar in the South Park Saloon, how to recognize avalanche territory, and how to deal with sloppy drunk Texas frat boys in our local watering holes during spring break.

We should all also know how to ice-skate. And we should all skate often. Yeah, there are some components of the sport that seem contrary to the High Country way of thinking. There is little speed in ice-skating for your average person. The only variation in terrain comes in the form of bumps, divots, and cracks. It's just you and this physically perplexing thing called "ice" on clear skyed twenty-below nights, when your nose hairs are freezing fast and the thought of a Keoki coffee or three always sounds mighty good.

Unless you are a competitive skater of whatever stripe, for ice-skating to be "fun," you have to be ready, willing, and able to escape into your own thoughts. You have to be able to get off on the simplicity of repetitive motion, of trying to make yourself feel relaxed and smooth at the same time that your mind goes completely off in whatever direction it wants and needs.

And, while that may not seem like the kind of activity likely to appeal to many people in this speed-crazed place in this speed-addicted time, ice-skating is an activity that produces, even if only for a few hours, a kind of mental state-of-being we could all use a lot more of here in the High Country.

The Fine Art of Giving Directions

It's one of those trailside memories that doesn't really get any better or funnier with age or subsequent re-tellings. I still want to choke the living crap out of the imbecile hombre who, one fine summer day fourteen years ago, committed the worst direction-giving faux pas I have ever witnessed or been party to. You can't really do any worse than a complete, 180-degree mistake when it comes to giving directions to someone out in the woods, and that's exactly what the guy did—to me and my buddies.

I was hiking the Appalachian Trail in 1979. There were four of us who had hooked up somewhere along the line and were hiking together for the then-time-being. We were a couple of miles from some mountain I don't remember the name of. What I do remember is that we had to ascend and descend that mountain before setting up camp for the night.

We passed three guys going the opposite direction, meaning they had just come from the place we were headed. As the seven of us stood there hobnobbing on the trail, we asked about the upcoming water availability. One of the three gentlemen told us, without compunction, that we would pass close by a pond before beginning our ascent. At the time of this conversation, we were standing right next to a small stream, where we could have easily filled our water bottles. But, armed with the pertinent skinny that we would, in less than an hour and before we began the day's last—and biggest—climb, pass by another water source, we passed on the close-at-hand stream in favor of the upcoming pond. We hiked what we thought was about the right distance. Then we hiked some more. Negatory on the pond. Shortly thereafter, we began our ascent, or should I say, we began our dry-as-a-bone ascent. By the time we reached the other side, several hours later, we all looked like that skeletal Far Side character whose misfortune it was to be crawling on his belly through Death Valley, all for the benefit of a Gary Larsen ha-ha.

Suddenly, we came upon, you guessed it, a pond.

So, not only did the SOB we had talked to on the trail give us information based upon his own direction-of-travel, rather than ours, but his two friends stood right there listening to him do it while nodding their heads in complete agreement. We had interfaced with a holy trinity of directional discombobulation.

I was pissed. I seriously gave thought to running those losers down so that I might lecture them on the depth and breadth of their complete and utter stupidity. We were all the more perplexed by our miscommunication because the three men-in-question had, during the course of our brief conversation, managed to brag about the fact that they had each just graduated from a prestigious university that, herein, shall remain nameless, lest it lose its accreditation as a result of this tale.

I've thought a lot over the years about that event specifically and about the important art of giving—and receiving—directions in general. Directions-giving, as well as the ability to impart and decipher nuances in the directions-giving/receiving process, is a mighty important skill in any outdoorsperson's communications repertoire. There are even circumstances where and when the ability to give or receive directions might have serious implications on the mortality front.

The result of those many years of direction-giving-related ponderment has been that I have evolved into one seriously anal-retentive humanoid in this context. This situation has been exacerbated by the fact that, for two and one-half years, I worked in the land surveying business, which is a trade that takes very seriously its directions-giving and taking. It has been further exacerbated by the fact that I even once wrote a guidebook, to an area where trail signs and, for that matter, trails, are few and far between—meaning I had to learn to be slightly creative, if not outright accurate, while dealing with how best to give directions to people who, in many cases, probably ought not be allowed outside alone, unless they are on a leash.

Based on mounds of related experience, on trail and off, I have come up with what I believe is a fairly digestible set of commandments regarding the very important art of giving and taking directions. These commandments, which have (admittedly) not yet been etched in stone by any deity I know of (but which shortly will be, if my celestial sources are correct), should not only be revered but, at the same time, considered to be the foundation of hundreds of thousands of potential trailside psychic bondings, the result of which will surely be legions of well-oriented, happy, un-thirsty hikers tromping through the woods in places like the High Country and Maine (particularly along the Appalachian Trail).

One more thing: directions, of course, can take several guises. One can be to tell a person how to actually get to a certain, usually trail-less, place. "This is how to get to the summit of Grizzly Peak." The other is to lay off-trail information on someone. "There's an unmarked spring about a hundred feet off the trail just this side of the snake pit." The following commandments, I feel, serve to handle both of these types of directions-giving themes.

When you are giving directions:

- Do not give directions to anyone unless asked. Even if you assume, for whatever reason or combinations of reasons, that the person you pass on the trail will get hopelessly lost the exact moment you part ways with them, that's their business, not yours. Let them do their own hike their own way.

- When you are asked directions, do not present a know-it-all demeanor. That will only distract the person you are talking to, and that's not the name of the directions-giving game. While you're acting like a modern-day John Muir describing how to get to the closest spring, they're spending more time thinking about what a butthead you are than they are about the fact that they need to take the right-hand fork in the trail two miles away.

- Do not automatically assume that you are dealing with a person who is on the same communications wave length as you. Such an assumption is tempting, because directions-related conversations generally take place in a mutually acceptable venue. But remember: just because you're talking to someone who, like you, is standing out in the woods in the rain while legions of mosquitoes tear at your skin with a nine-hundred-pound pack on your back that you have anything, communications-wise, in common. Quite the contrary. In all likelihood, one of you is a Mac, while the other is a PC. Your job is to develop a common directions-oriented language. Call it the ASCII of the woods.
- Different people use different cues and keys upon which to base conceptions of reality. Since the person you are giving directions to likely has no familiarity whatsoever with the place you are describing, whether it be the best campsite in twelve states or a side trail to the only spring for fifteen miles, make yourself clear. After all, if they are familiar with the area, they likely wouldn't be asking you for directions.

  Some people really need physical references when they're processing conceptual information. They want and need to hear about where the rotted corduroy bridge crossing the bog will fit into the directions you are laying on them. Others want and need time and distance information. You should be able to tell from the questions they ask which kinds of references you ought to be using while giving directions. Of course, depending on the way you personally process information, you might be more inclined to remember physical points-of-reference than you are time and distance, or vice-versa.
- Do not muddy up the direction-giving waters by tossing in tons of extraneous information. If you're telling someone that they will come to a stream just the other side of the boulder field about three miles up the valley, there's no reason whatsoever to toss in references to the open meadow with the nineteen species of wildflowers blooming, the cliff and the gum wrapper lying in the middle of the trail they will pass along the way.

At the same time, though, try to ascertain if the person/people you are giving directions to are outdoors neophytes and/or nimwits. The longer the distance involved in the directions you are giving, the more nervous inexperienced people will become that they have not rubbed elbows with a landmark you described to them. So, if you're telling a group of obvious greenhorns how to get to a place twelve miles away, toss in a landmark or two every couple of miles. If you do not, you can bet the farm the people on the receiving end of your directions will start getting a tad nervous after a few hours of not seeing something you told them about. They will, after a while, begin to think that maybe you, through incompetence or purposeful malice, led them astray, and that you are now sitting in a watering hole somewhere regaling your amigos with the story about how you sent a troop of people you passed on the trail in a completely wrong direction.

- I am a firm believer in accenting directions-giving with body language. Now, you have to be careful that your hand motions and general physical English don't get too distracting. But, while you're telling someone how to get to the unmarked spring near Reed's Peak in New Mexico's Aldo Leopold Wilderness, it doesn't hurt to replicate the S-turn on the side trail just above the spring with a little hand and arm motion. The thing is, make certain, when you're doing all this, that your hand motions aren't taken too literally. You may be pointing in a certain direction that is more relative to the verbal part of your directions-giving than it is to terra firma-based reality. That's okay, but just make certain the person you are talking to understands this.

- If you're really on a roll, pull out a map with the idea of making your descriptions relative to on-map landmarks.

- If you do not know how to get somewhere, admit it, even if you are being begged for information from some doe-eyed sweet young thing that clearly needs your help and is willing to pay for it.

- Try to not describe directions to two places. If you come across a party that wants to know the best way to get to the summit of Mount Yale, at the same time they want to know how to descend from the summit to Brown's Cabin (both in Colorado's Collegiate Peaks Wilderness), then lay the directions to the summit on one member of the party, then lay the directions to Brown's Cabin on another member of the party.
- Do not assume that the member of the party you are giving directions to who acts like the most-together member of the group is the most-together member of the group.
- Do not overlook the possibility of stepping into a nearby clearing and actually pointing out to the person you are giving directions to where they need to go.
- Remember, if the party you are talking to is going the opposite direction, you need to flip-flop your information.

Many of the same observations about receiving directions obviously are the same as those applying to giving directions:

- You will often need to coax information out of people on the side of the trail, especially if the people are not as experienced as you. Inexperienced outdoorspeople may not understand what information you need or want. Again, remember that the person giving directions might be inclined to talk about distance/time, while you might prefer information about landmarks. The more you understand about how you personally process directional information, the better. Then, steer the fountain of information you are drinking from on the side of the trail in the direction that makes you most comfortable.
- Attempt to ascertain ASAP if the person giving you directions has his orientational ducks in a huddle. A quick, "Would that be going north or south on the trail?" now can save a lot of foul-mooded anguish later.
- Do not hesitate to write stuff down. If nothing else, written directions can later be used as evidence in a court of law after

you have hunted down someone who laid the wrong skinny on you and killed him or her. When all else fails, have the person giving you directions draw a map in the dirt.

- Keep a smile on your face. After all, it is you who are responsible for yourself while in the woods. Directions from another hiker are handy, but you should not come to rely upon such information to get your ass into and out of the woods safely. Neither should you base a decision on whether or not to fill your water bottles on any assurances that there is another water supply right up the trail. If you do, you'll end up becoming a crotchety old fart who can't let go of a bad memory that happened fourteen years ago.

Flyfishing as a Metaphor of Life?

The other day, while on my way with several other folks to climb a fourteener, the subject of flyfishing came up. The way it came up was something along the lines of:

Driver of car (who your not-so-humble narrator hardly knows): So, M. John, where's your favorite place to flyfish?

M. John: I would rather castrate myself than ever hold any manner of fishing equipage, unless it be to toss that equipage into a dirty-diaper-filled dumpster.

Driver of car (incredulously): Well, M. John, you must have never tried *flyfishing*.

M. John: That is correct. But I have been in the presence of many flyfishers, both while they were flyfishing and while they were hob-nobbing about flyfishing. Also, I have done just about every other kind of fishing, so I believe I have enough of a handle on the wheres, whys, and how-tos of flyfishing that I am able to say, knowing myself as well as I do, that I would rather castrate myself than etc., etc.

Knowing myself as well as I do and as well as I already said I do, I understand there are plenty of bad-family-memory reasons why I loathe the entire concept of fishing. I spent more time fishing as a youngster than just about anyone I have ever talked to or even heard about. When we lived in the Adirondacks, we spin-casted the Ausable and Saranac rivers until our heads spun more than our lures. While living in central Kentucky, we trolled for such monstrous game fish as crappie and blue gill in the stagnant lakes thereabouts in a small aluminum boat, while the smell of mosquito repellent wafted around us like a sewage-based perfume. And, while living on the Chesapeake Bay in Virginia, we fished for monsters of the ocean deep, often catching creatures so ugly and mean-looking that we would flip a coin, and the loser had to remove the beast from the hook. I have also surf-casted on North Carolina's Outer Banks and have done some grade-B deep sea fishing off of Cabo San Lucas.

And, with the exception of the Cabo San Lucas experience, which was decidedly alcohol-influenced, every single one of those aforesaid fishing experiences was stirred by something far more evil and deadly and vile than alcohol: parental mandate. Yessirree, Bob and Bob-ette, my parents were firm believers in the psychological benefits that were, in their minds, unarguably to be derived from engaging in a battle of wits with fish. Consequently, every single non-winter Sunday of my entire miserable pre-eighteen life was spent rod-in-hand.

I have been fishing exactly twice since the exact second I entered adulthood. The first was my Cabo experience, and the second was not out of any desire to fish but, rather, a desire to please my stepfather, who, like many people before and after him, would rather fish than do anything else in the world, except maybe work in the garden (another activity that makes me want to run screaming into the night).

So, the foundation of my anti-fishing psychological edifice was dug during the dark days of youth, when fishing was not a form of recreation but, rather, a form of punishment, except that I never could figure out what I was being punished for.

Now, here I am neck-deep in a part of the country where, for a number of reasons—such as the fact that many flyfishing devotees are/were great writers (David Quamman, Randy Wayne Wright, John Gierach, the late Norman MacLean)—flyfishing has gained a place in the outdoor recreation pantheon that, like climbing and downhill skiing, borders on religion.

And I cannot, for the life of me, figure out why.

I have, in the course of (1) being a normal, fairly inquisitive human being who happens to detest fishing, and (2) a writer who writes a lot about outdoors kinda things and happens to detest fishing, asked a fair number of people why they would rather be flyfishing than, say, going for a walk in the woods (or, for that matter, eye-dropping battery acid onto their pupils). The answers are actually fairly uniform and are generally the same as answers to any "Why do you do this particular outdoor-oriented form of activity?"-type queries. Except, with flyfishers, as opposed to, say, rock climbers or bird watchers, there's always a hint of "You can't *possibly* understand without giving it a whirl" in their responses. I am often told that flyfishing is a good excuse to get outside, along a river, in the sunshine. Well, so is walking or, for that matter, lying on a river bank, drinking a beer, reading a book, and/or making love.

I have been told that flyfishing is a wonderful opportunity to learn heapin' helpin's of important stuff about the natural world, especially entomology and the inner workings of riparian habitats. Well, it seems to me that such cranial endeavors, should one be so disposed to embark upon them, could be more easily achieved without having to worry about toting $1,000 worth of gear through the willows and, then, spending hours upon hours trying to catch fish that will, upon being landed, almost immediately be released.

Trout have to have some mighty serious perplexedness regarding the catch-and-release consciousness that pervades, nay, dominates, the flyfishing world. If trout are even half as smart as those who spend vast amounts of time trying to catch them—and I believe they are *at least* half as smart—then they ought to have a fairly substantial instinctual comprehension regarding the predator/prey thing, or else they wouldn't have so much trepidation when it comes to going after the fake flies that flyfishers dangle before their (the trouts') noses. If this were not the case, flyfishers could simply dangle Vienna sausages on a string in front of your average trout, and they (once again, the trout) would go into an immediate Vienna sausage feeding frenzy, which would leave a lot of flytiers out of work, but it would do wonders for the sagging Vienna sausage industry. Once they (the trout, though, from what I hear, it can often be the flyfisher) are hooked, they probably think something like, "Well, Ernie, you screwed up big time this fine day, and now you're going to pay the price: you're gonna be some flyfisher's din-din. Then, all of a sudden, while Ernie's trout life is flashing before him, while he's pondering a long list of trout imponderables, such as the indiscretions he committed while he was a mere fingerling, wondering what the trout afterlife will be like (will I come back as something else, mayhaps a flyfisher, or will I just dissolve into nothingness and, either way, will it make any spiritual difference that my intestines, head, fins, and scales will be left in the woods like so much organic flotsam, while the rest of me is taken back to Denver, wrapped in aluminum foil, placed in the freezer and, sometime in the distant future, cooked in lemon?) when, suddenly, for no apparent good reason, Ernie is simply released, with nothing more than a sore mouth and the memory of seeing a bright white light at the end of a long tunnel, while voices from his past whispered, "Ernie, it's all right, you're coming home."

I mean, what a trout mind-fuck.

I guess—from a superior point-of-view—that is the main context in which I frame my feelings about flyfishing in the politically correct '90s. Basically, I believe flyfishing is about as frivolous an undertaking as can be undertaken. It is harmless enough, in and of itself, and a very good way to keep track of the types of people who would be inclined to flyfish.

But, when viewed philosophically, I believe flyfishing borders on bonafide weird. Under the guise of making a serious attempt to bond with Mother Nature, flyfishing is little more than another in a long line of ways that humankind attempts to assert its mastery over the natural world. I mean, what on earth besides that would possess anyone to want to snare a trout, only to let it go?

I understand (who could not?) that the MacLean-esque, flyfishing-as-a-metaphor-of-and-for-life school of thought is tres chic (to the point of inflicting nausea on the innocent masses) these days. (Witness any copy of *Outside* magazine). I should also note that the book, *A River Runs Through It,* was wonderful, and the movie of the same name was one of my very favorites, so it's not like I feel that the very concept of flyfishing soils everything it touches. And, perhaps that's my biggest complaint about the entire activity.

I hate outdoorsy trends, especially those that are based upon the sociology of tres-chic-ness. Like fourteener bagging, flyfishing seems to be washing over the High Country landscape like a major break in the levy of sanity. The comparison with fourteener bagging is, I believe, a fairly good one. People who are looking to "bag" fourteeners (much like flyfishers "bag" trout) often do so despite poor aesthetics. It matters not that there are generally dozens of people atop any fourteener at any given time. It matters not that, a mere mile away from a fourteener summit might lie a beautiful, lonesome mountain that stands a mere 13,990 feet high. Fourteener bagging is the trend, so let's get on with it.

When I see a dozen folks flyfishing on the Blue River alongside I-70 behind the Factory Outlet Stores in Silverthorne, Colorado, I know that I'm dealing with outdoorspeople who truly have a handle on every one of the philosophical and metaphorical aspects of their sport and, by extension, the entire natural world.

Right.

What I really see is people caught up in the tidal wave of recreational fad, what my friend Tom Jones Jr. calls "a trend runs through it." Yeah, yeah, yeah, I know there are fair numbers of people like my friend Dan Bell (owner of Columbine Outfitters in Frisco) who have dialed into flyfishing in ways other people haven't and couldn't even if they opened their minds and tried. And, because of Dan's dialed-into-it-ness, the world, on some level, is truly a richer place.

But, for the most part, for most people, flyfishing is so inconsequential that the only comment it merits is a long-winded screed like this one. Anyone who needs to score $1,000 worth of fishing gear and then bother the hell out of trout in order to have an excuse to rub elbows with the great out-of-doors and/or to interface with an outdoors-induced meditative/philosophical state of mind ought to simply stay indoors, where, perhaps, they could set up an aquarium, get stoned, and watch the little fishies pass to and fro, to and fro.

Survival

There are few things funnier in the world than listening to one of your buddies telling an "I-almost-died-while-out-in-the-woods" kinda survival story. Most times, everyone in the room, even while enjoying the yarn, sort of rolls their joint and several eyes and operates, from a listener's perspective, with the full understanding that most likely some event-enhancement is going on, which is fine, because everyone who finds themselves in what they perceive as a potentially life-threatening situation is allowed at least a modicum of leeway when it comes time to recount the tale to one's chums.

The best way to decide what, if any, truth is coming through in the storytelling is to determine whether or not, if the events being described had happened to you, would you tell anyone about them, or would you just go through life with your lips sealed tight, hoping against hope that no one ever learned of your misadventure, lest you gain a reputation for being a biological hybrid between a moron and a loser. If the answer to that determination is a resounding, "Mum would be the word if that was my story," then, mayhaps, there is a kernel of non-exaggeration, non-lying, and non-chronological manipulation at work in the story telling.

A buddy of mine recently laid such a tale on me and, though I don't believe he was telling me the whole truth and nothing but the truth, there was enough in the way of "Boy, if I'd a found myself in those circumstances, I wouldn't even tell the story to *myself*, lest someone overhear me" going on in my brain that I tended to believe the bulk of the tale. And, as funny and improbable as the story was, it got me thinking about the concept of survival in general and emergency survival gear specifically.

What happened, basically, is this: a very good friend of mine who, though a suburban dweller and a member in good stead of a profession that one does not ordinarily associate with prowess in the great out-of-doors, happens to be fairly experienced in the backcountry (I even made his acquaintance on the trail in the boondocks of Mexico), managed to get about four months off of work. His plan, which kicked off in mid-May 1993, was to travel throughout the Mountain Time Zone, stopping hither and yon as he felt like it to hike and camp. The only thing was, since the Mountain Time Zone got a ton of snow during the winter of 1993, he would have to start his trip out in the deep southwest of New Mexico, where there was little snow on the ground in mid-May.

This was a part of the country that my friend was not overly familiar with and, thus, he bought a map of the Gila National Forest and basically picked a trail out at random, drove a gazillion miles down a nasty and wonderful four-wheel-drive road, parked his truck, cinched his pack down, and hit the trail.

The thing is, even though that particular part of New Mexico—the Aldo Leopold Wilderness—is surprisingly alpine in nature, with elevations topping out at 10,000 feet, it is remarkably dry. One pretty much has to know where the few springs are, lest one wither away with a parched and swollen tongue protruding from one's mouth. After a day of nursing a mere two liters of water, my buddy decided to leave his gear in camp and dayhike back to a place he had been several days before, a place where he knew there was a spring, in order to replenish his meager water supply, which, by that time, consisted mostly of spit on and around a tongue that was rapidly becoming parched and swollen and was beginning to protrude from his mouth.

That place was about eight miles back, so my buddy left camp early, figuring he would be back to his tent well before dark. He hiked back to the spring, per his plan, then turned around to hike back to his camp. Somewhere along the line, he lost track of the trail back to his tent, or, more accurately, he got waylaid on a different trail. He spent two full days looking for the right trail and, thus, for his gear. He failed, which is so funny I still wake up at least twice a week in the middle of the night laughing about it.

After two days of bivouacking, he finally threw in the towel and hiked out an anonymous drainage until he stumbled onto the only dirt road for fifty miles. He eventually hitched back to his truck, where he had some spare gear. After resting up for a day and consulting some local rangers, he cinched on his backup backpack and went back into the woods with the intent of salvaging his lost gear.

He spent two more days looking—again, to no avail. Somewhere up along the spine of the Black Range, there's a Northface tent and pack, a cook kit, a Sierra Designs sleeping bag, a Therm-a-Rest pad, and an MSR stove just hanging out, abandoned. Though the tent, which was left set up, and the pack, which was left inside the tent with a food bag in it, has surely been invaded by hungry critters, the rest of the gear is likely just sitting there in the woods, wondering where daddy is and when he's coming back. Well, daddy's back home in the Upper Midwest right now, and though the thought of that lost gear will likely never again leave his psyche, he swears he ain't never goin' back to the Aldo Leopold Wilderness. Not for gear; not for nothin'.

What all this amounts to is this: my buddy, along about his second day of stumbling through the woods, came to the conclusion that he had better get out of the mountains that very night, lest he expire. He was dehydrated and virtually foodless. The only thing that saved his carcass was the fact that, typical of his anal-retentive Michigan upbringing, he was extremely organized, even while he was in the process of losing a thousand-or-so beans worth of gear in the woods.

When he left his gear behind to seek water, he carried his daypack, which contained a fair amount of the kind of cheesy "survival gear" that one sees for sale in the Wal-Mart outdoor section or at hunting equipment stores. He carried a $5 space blanket, a $3 nylon poncho, a couple of extra candy bars, matches in one of those twinky little plastic match holders, iodine tablets, a small first-aid kit, a map, and compass, and a key ring flashlight. All of which sounds like a lot, but actually weighs only a couple of pounds.

My buddy credits that survival gear with saving his life. He wrapped up in front of a small fire at night in the space blanket and poncho and didn't die of hypothermia, even though he experienced both freezing rain and snow. He was able to purify and consume even the foulest stock pond water, which boasts more disease-making microscopic organisms than you can shake a stick at, because he had his iodine. Once he decided to punt looking for his gear, he was able to stumble out of the woods because he had a map and compass. Etc., etc.

Yesterday, I took out on the kind of dayhike that I take out on about one hundred times a year. I went up to the base of Eccles Pass and returned to the Meadow Creek Trail parking lot. In my fanny pack, I carried exactly two water bottles and a windbreaker.

Last Sunday, I hiked up Mount Huron, a fourteener, with my wife and two friends. Between us, we were carrying less survival gear than my buddy was carrying when he was bumbling through the New Mexico woods like a New Yorker on Quaaludes.

When you live in the High Country, you get to thinking of yourself as correctly oriented when it comes to taking care of yourself in the woods. On some probably undeserved level, you get to thinking you will recognize potentially adverse conditions and either successfully avoid them or somehow tough it out as those conditions manifest themselves in your Here & Now.

This attitude is especially poignant in the realm of fourteener bagging. A high percentage of people you see on fourteeners these days carry only small fanny packs with a sandwich and jacket, like, if a summer blizzard suddenly blew in, that would be enough to survive, because, you know, we're all bad-ass Coloradans.

Well, I've now learned a lesson from my Michigan buddy, who, I'm absolutely certain, if you told him he would one day lose a bunch of gear in the woods, would tell you you were nuts.

I'm going to cruise on by Wal-Mart at my earliest convenience, which, I believe, might be sometime this afternoon. I'm gonna score me two sets of that cheesy survival gear in their outdoor section—one for my wife and one for yours truly. And I plan to put mine in my fanny pack, and the next time I hike to Eccles Pass or up a fourteener, I will have it with me, just in case.

That may set me at functional, as well as philosophical, odds with many of my fourteener-bagging brethren, who might come to view me on some level as an outdoors twink. But, that's okay. At least when we're all sitting around the campfire telling "I-almost-died-while-out-in-woods" stories, mine will, hopefully, consist of nothing but out-and-out exaggerations, lies, and overt chronological manipulations.

Which is the way it should be.

CLOSE 'EM DOWN

I've found myself at the epicenter of a few more barroom confrontations than I care to remember and, needless to say, a fair number of those unfortunate confrontations have come about because of differences of opinion regarding various and sundry wilderness/wilderness use-oriented issues.

Almost without fail, these disagreements have centered around the philosophical abyss that often separates my naturally argumentative environmental self from the smelly, uncouth, and uncultured (and, all too often, un-small) minions of Earth-plundering offenders: loggers, miners, ATVers, ORVers, real estate developers, hunters, cattlemen et al.

But, strange to say, the most tense situation over which I ever found myself heading posthaste towards the rear exit of a watering hole occurred not because I had boisterously referred to, say, some geek hunters as weenified killers of defenseless critters or anything but, rather, when I had, in print, made a proposal that I had mistakenly believed would raise me to the status of cult hero among the local environmental community.

I was wrong. Way wrong. Humorously wrong.

The situation was this: in the early '80s, the Forest Service instigated a permit system for the Indian Peaks Wilderness, located just south of Rocky Mountain National Park. When that decision was made, the Indian Peaks became the first legally designated wilderness area in Colorado wherein paperwork would be required for summertime camping. Great. All I would have to do to camp in the Indian Peaks, which is a beautiful, though small (73,391 acres) wilderness area that straddles a particularly rugged part of the Continental Divide, would be to slide on down to Datatix, pull out my Visa card, and get me a ticket. While I was there, you know, I could look into details about the next Hulk-a-mania extravaganza. Really enhances that ol' wilderness feeling. (This, I'll concede, is a tad overly dramatic. In reality, Datatix, or some such business, does, indeed, sell tickets/permits to the Indian Peaks. But, they are also available, at little or no cost, from several ranger stations.)

The reason the Forest Service instigated a permit system for the Indian Peaks was, not surprisingly, severe overuse. According to Forest Service employees I talked with, the Indian Peaks was being Vibram-soled, fire-circled, and human-feced near-bouts to death. Clearly, something had to be done, and the only alternative available, in the minds of the Forest Service powers that be, was to attempt to restrict camping (the highest-impact form of wilderness use) by requiring permits (which would be limited in number) to camp from June till September. (Day-use in the summer and all kinds of use during the off-season do not require permits.)

The main problem was—is—that, even with a strict permit system in place and enforced, it will take the Indian Peaks at least fifty years to recover from the overuse that necessitated the permit system in the first place. I asked a couple of Forest Service people how long it would take for the Indian Peaks to recover if the area was simply closed to *all* backcountry use. They could only guess, because they had never thought of that as an alternative. They said maybe only ten to fifteen years. Ding ding ding.

I was working for a small newspaper in Granby, located in the county that borders the Indian Peaks to the west, and I wrote a column that said, in no uncertain terms, that "we" users of the backcountry ought to be ashamed of ourselves every time we looked east towards the Indian Peaks. This was, in my not-so-humble opinion, a clear example of wilderness enthusiasts fouling their own nest and, except in the most-grand overview of life on Earth in the late twentieth century, the dark and evil forces of the techno-industrial complex could not be blamed for this sad state of affairs. "They" didn't erode the trails in the Indian Peaks. "They" didn't make the campsites bare and foul the streams. We did, and I felt very strongly that we ought to be doing something about it in the most direct sense.

I proposed in my column that the Indian Peaks simply be closed down for a decade or two, while it recovered from the transgressions of mankind. I argued that anyone who truly loves the wilderness in general and the Indian Peaks in particular, would only be too happy to agree to such a plan.

I expected trouble, and got it, from the local business community, which relies heavily on tourists, many of whom venture to that part of Colorado specifically to visit the Indian Peaks. The local chamber of commerce types argued vehemently that, if the Indian Peaks was closed, many potential visitors would simply take their dollars elsewhere. What I most certainly did not expect was the venomous reaction I received from many backcountry enthusiasts. Quite the contrary. I expected to have a lifetime's worth of carbonated beverages purchased for me by people who I "thought" (and, in retrospect, I use that word very loosely) would reluctantly, sadly, agree that, yes, if we are going to strut through life bearing the environmental banner, then, by gods, we ought to be willing to make sacrifices such as foregoing Indian Peaks forays for a few years, if that's what it takes to make this little piece of the planet a better place.

After all, it's not like closing the Indian Peaks would have condemned us to playing putt-putt and shuffleboard until such time as that particular wilderness area was re-opened, rejuvenated. Right in our backyards, we had Rocky Mountain National Park, the Never Summer Wilderness, the Rawah Wilderness, and hundreds of thousands of acres of nonwilderness national forest land in which to hike, mountain bike, kayak, backcountry ski, and run naked through the wildflowers.

Yet, my erstwhile wilderness-loving philosophical compadres were, after reading my column, ready and willing, en masse, to kick my ass all over town because I had proposed that, effectively, one of their favorite playgrounds be closed off to them and their recreational pursuits. I was stunned. And, ten years later, I still am stunned, because it is becoming clearer and clearer that such extreme action is needed not only in the Indian Peaks, but in many other parks and wilderness areas nationwide.

The foundation of this argument is based upon my belief—and I have journalistically rubbed elbows with the wording of the 1964 Wilderness Act once or twice—that legally designated wilderness areas exist secondarily as backcountry recreational areas for those of us who prefer to twiddle our thumbs far away from civilization as often as possible. They exist primarily as habitat protection for the animals and plants that need untrammeled areas in order to survive, as individuals and as species. We should be allowed to visit wilderness areas only so long as we don't screw them up too badly. And, when we do, the appropriate governmental agency should simply close them down. Build a high-voltage electric fence around them until all is mended and all is well. Then re-open them at the appropriate time with an Israeli-border-crossing-like mentality permit system—complete with thorough background and luggage checks. There is precedent—albeit not large scale—for this proposal. The Whiteoak Trail in Shanandoah National Park was once closed down because of overuse. As well, most of Mesa Verde National Park's backcountry is off limits to visitors, though I understand that has more to do with archeological concerns than it does with concerns about the environment. And many of the new national parks in Central America only allow human visitation in certain small areas. What's left is left for the wildlife. Even Sir Edmund Hillary has proposed closing Everest down for twenty-five years, at least partially to grant the world's highest peak a recovery period.

It may certainly be argued that, with more foresightful planning on the part of our governmental land steward agencies, as well as by backcountry users, we could, before the fact, eliminate the need for consideration of this admittedly drastic proposal. But, sad to say (and as we all know), the Interior and Agriculture departments are, policy-wise, very reactionary in nature. These entities identify problems only after they have become problems and, even then, they do not often react to those problems by taking stands strong enough to remedy the situation. These governmental entities are fans of "mitigations" rather than "solutions."

I understand that the argument can be made, based, if nothing else, on my own arguments, that we should close down all wilderness areas and limit our outdoor experiences to KOAs next to the interstate in rural Kansas so the marmots can do whatever it is that marmots do in absolute privacy. After all, many people would contend, with ample justification, that any amount of human interaction with wilderness areas brings with it some degree of negative impact. Even if that is the case, it would still not make for a strong enough argument for closing down all wilderness areas to, for example, me and my drinking buddies.

What I'm advocating is reasonable balance. There are clearly examples of wilderness/backcountry areas that are so overused that no other option, save closing them down for a while, is reasonable. Yet, I have never heard any major environmental organization put this option forth. And, I'm afraid, were any organization to do so, the resultant furor would transcend the usual environmentalist versus non-environmentalist battle lines. As my experience writing about the Indian Peaks Wilderness has shown, too many of us who would gladly risk a barroom brawl in the name of increased wilderness protection and designations cruise through life with a skewed perception of what wilderness areas are really for in the first place.

The Barbecue Odyssey

It had been at least six years since I last barbecued. My wife and I were, at one time, the proud owners of a lovely little $6 barbecuing device that boasted a lifetime guarantee that apparently covered not the lifetime of the grill but, rather, the lifetime of a mayfly. Coincidentally, about the time this fine example of American engineering burned through on the bottom—about the third time we used it—I decided, for completely unrelated reasons, to become a vegetarian, a state of being which I maintained for three and one-half years. During that time, it seemed somewhat imprudent to invest in a new grill as, let's face it, the notion of barbecuing non-flesh items is not as tantalizing as barbecuing, say, brats. Being unenticed by barbecued broccoli, Gay and I drifted farther and farther away from barbecued anything.

It seems, though, the longer we dwell in the High Country, the more Gay and I search out and embrace any and all things even vaguely associated with summer in places that have a more traditional definition of summer. We have toyed with the idea of buying a set of horseshoes, for instance. Or a croquet set.

But, since barbecuing seems to be undergoing a popularity explosion these days among the mountain jocks and jockettes we associate with, we opted, one day last spring, to keep up with the barbecuing Joneses. We decided to jump out of the wok and into the charcoal.

It was a beautiful spring Sunday morning when we walked into our local Wal-Mart with the specific intention of buying all the barbecuing equipage two people could ever possibly want or need.

This was more complicated than we had suspected, proving, once again, how far removed we, personally, are from mainstream American thought and action. (I mean, there's no way on Earth that someone of my advanced years who dwells in, say, central Ohio would think that any component of the barbecuing, or barbecue-equipment-procuring, process would be anything save a normal part of existence. To us, a written account of the entire experience should be included, after the fact, in the Old Testament, alongside Exodus.)

First, we had "thought" there would be three different kinds of grills to peruse, max. And we "thought" the main differences between those three hypothetical grills would be centered upon size.

Negatory.

Certainly, grills come in many sizes, covering the gamut from slightly larger than a fast-food hamburger, all the way up to the point where an entire cow could comfortably kick back on the grill part of the grill and still have room for a garnish of several hundred ears of corn.

Size, though, when you're talking in terms of grills, means more than simple surface area. There is also the height question to consider. To say nothing of shape. We never could figure out what the functional difference would be between a round grill and a square one, and the one Wal-Mart employee we asked simply looked at us funny and backed away slowly and cautiously.

As well, off in the techno-junkie region of Wal-Mart's grill province, there were three or four models that actually boasted dials and gauges and attached beverage holders and such and, thus, cost around $200. We could not envision becoming aficionados of outside meat cooking to the degree that we would actually be interested in trying to figure out what those dials and gauges were for, much less attempt to learn to use them. After all, that would likely mean having to barbecue sober, a thought we simply can't abide by.

As a last concern, there were actually fuel choices to ponder. Back in days of yore, people did not have to give so much as a moment's thought to fuel-oriented specifics about barbecuing. There was basically a choice of using charcoal-burning grills or cooking inside, on the stove. Of course, there was also Nixon in the White House during those otherwise simple times, so I'm not claiming they were Nirvanic.

Anyhow, we pretty much decided immediately to pass on the propane, butane, and nuclear fusion fuel options. (Call us purists.)

Along about this time, the maleness part of my male self was making a genuine effort to come to the confusion rescue. After all, for reasons I have never figured out, barbecuing has evolved into a particularly male activity. Did cavemen, back in cavemen days, push the tribe's females out of the way when it came time to barbecue mastodon burgers? This is not to say females never barbecue. My mother, for instance, was one of the best barbecuers I ever knew. It is to say that, by and large, males elbow their way to the front and center of the barbecuing process and, by and large, females, intelligently, let them.

So, while I was standing there in Wal-Mart, I started thinking I should know much more about this grill-buying endeavor than I did because, after all, as the resident male in my marital situation, I was supposed to have a grip on barbecuing-pertinent skinny. I, sad to say, did not. Is it proper, I wondered, to kick the tires on a grill? Is there an owner's manual I could check out? How about a test drive?

After much head-scratching and looking at each other and shrugging, hoping the other one would have some sort of constructive input on the matter, we decided to buy a "table-top" rectangular model, partially because it cost only $18 (it was the second-cheapest one) and partially because it would fit into the back of our Subaru while still allowing enough room for us.

On our hand-in-hand, marital bliss-like way out of Wal-Mart, we couldn't help feeling that we had forgotten something—something maybe even critical to the health and well-being of our upcoming barbecuing operation. Then it hit us . . . charcoal. So, we scurry back to the charcoal part of the store—which covered an entire wall—only to learn that we had to make a choice here, as well. There's your basic "charcoal" kinda charcoal, your "match-light" kinda charcoal, and your "smoke-specific" kinda charcoal, like mesquite-flavored and hickory-scented.

We went with the mesquite-scented match-light stuff, because (1) it seemed simpler (we wouldn't have to buy charcoal-lighting fluid) and

(2) we were starting to get a headache and, therefore, all of a sudden, wanted this grill-procurement process to be over and done with ASAP, no offense to the ambiance of Wal-Mart on a pretty Sunday morning.

Okay, now that we were armed with all the requisite hardware, it was off to Safeway for a little chow.

We had decided well before the fact to keep this inaugural foray down barbecue lane on the embarrassingly uncreative side: corn on the cob and some cow meat would do us just fine. So, we simply sashayed over to the veggie section and choose four ears of prime-looking corn. This took about point-two seconds. At long last, we were on a roll. On our way over to the other side of the store, however, we made the mistake of wandering down the ketchup, mustard, and mayonnaise aisle, which, from the sidelines, seems innocuous enough. And it would have been, except that, halfway down the aisle, I compounded the mistake by looking to the left. And there they were: 250,000 different kinds of barbecue sauce. Who would have thought? We were no longer on a roll.

So, here we are expecting simplicity incarnate and, instead, we are faced with another in a long line of barbecue-oriented consumer Rubik's Cubes.

First, we have to decide if we really want barbecue sauce in the first place. We don't have a frigging clue. Maybe we would prefer to let the dead creature we planned on hooving several hours later speak for itself, flavor-wise. We don't really remember what barbecue sauce tastes like. We hobnob and hem and haw, all the time wistfully mentally harkening back to those blissfully simple days of vegetarianism. Twelve years later, we decided, yes, we'll go the sauce route.

Which meant, of course, that we had to choose a sauce phylum, class, order, and species. We finally decide upon K.C. Masterpiece, because we have at least heard of that brand, though we can't recollect between us what it is we heard about it. Perhaps it is manufactured by fascists and contains nasal excretions or something. We opt for a medium-sized bottle, because we can't make a committed decision regarding small (in case it tastes like shit) or large (because it's more economical).

Then, we had to choose what flavor we would like. This causes some degree of consternation, because we wonder if we are supposed to try to coordinate the flavor of the sauce with the smoke scent of the charcoal we bought earlier. After all, we have no interest in committing a barbecue faux pas right off the bat. In the interest of avoiding a clashing of mostly artificial flavors, we go for the mesquite-flavored sauce to complement our mesquite-flavored charcoal—hoping against hope that we were not going to enter the realm of over-bearingness on the mesquite front.

Now, it's time for the culinary coup de grace: the animal flesh. There's no doubt we are headed directamundo to the steak section. At least this much we determined before the fact. As we were making our way past the chicken, ground beef, tripe, liver, and pork chops, scant feet away from our destination, sad to say, it dawns on us that, maybe, some kinds of cow are better-suited for barbecuing than others. Damn. But—wait!—Gay's eyes spy several specific cuts sporting little "This Kind of Meat Barbecues Might Fine" stickers. We are saved! We snag what seems like the appropriate acreage, and we are finally off, homeward bound, drooling good, clean, all-American, hyper-expectant, carnivorous drool all over ourselves.

So, now we're home, and we realize, after opening the box with the grill in it, that we have not opened a box with a grill in it at all. Rather, we have opened a box with sixty trillion grill parts in it. I suddenly regret having started working on the celebratory tequila so early. By the time the sun starts nipping at the crest of the Ten Mile Range, the grill parts have been bent, hammered, and otherwise coerced into a seemingly functional unit. We pull out a camera and photograph ourselves, with our arms proudly around the grill, which we have named, "HAL- 9000."

Now is the moment of truth. It's time to fire HAL up. We make what seems like an educated guess regarding the number of charcoal charks, or whatever the hell it is you call pieces of charcoal, and we're off. One match, and this matchlight stuff, as advertised, starts cooking almost as good as a stove, which, if we had used instead of this new grill, we would have finished eating hours ago.

As the charks begin their mystifying journey from mere black lumps to red-hot forms of combustion, I reflect upon the fact that at one time in my life, I was actually a fairly expert barbecuist. I lived in a boondock little town in the swamplands of eastern Virginia, in an old, rambling house on the Severn River that had a wonderful, huge screened porch. A perfect barbecue venue.

There were about four or five couples that would get together, literally, late every Saturday afternoon for a barbecue-centered party marathon that rarely ended before 2 AM, when the hot, sticky, mosquito-infested southern summer night would give way somewhat to the dank coolness of early morning. These evenings would typically end with some old Leonard Cohen or Leo Kottke tunes playing low on the stereo, with us altering our consciousness appropriately, while the Severn's muddy waters lapped forty-feet away and our stomachs grumbled through the long, tedious process of digesting large quantities of barbecued meat, which was consumed with enthusiasm and all the fixin's, like cole slaw, rolls, corn, and home-grown marijuana.

That was the last place I lived in my home county before moving to the West, never to return East, except for brief and infrequent visits. Among the few positive memories I retain about the East in general and Gloucester County, Virginia, specifically, are those exquisite multi-hour barbecue parties. I remember the bonding of the guys as we all stood around the grill, hands in pockets, smoke in eyes, talking sports, and basically setting the stage for future Dockers commercials. I remember sitting naked with my girlfriend out in our two-person rubber raft, which was tied to our rickety old dock, while the smell of cooking burgers or dogs wafted out over the river. I remember the horseshoes and the badminton and, yes, even the croquet. I remember my best buddy, Norb, spending hours every Saturday evening making gallons and gallons of his world-famous blackberry ice cream.

As idyllic as I try to make those barbecue evenings sound, the main reason we gathered on my porch every Saturday was overt boredom. We lived in such a geedunk little craphole there was nothing else to do in the way of recreation and, even if there was, our destitute college student butts could not have afforded to do it. But, how we handle boredom, as individuals and a society, speaks directly to who we are. And we handled our boredom by getting together regularly for barbecues with our closest amigos, as if we sensed that it wouldn't be much longer before we all went our separate ways. Which is exactly what happened and, basically, we have never gotten back together again. I don't believe there is symbolism in that fact, but maybe there is. And, if there is, maybe one day I will see it, come to understand it, and do something about it.

When I moved West in 1975, I premeditatedly left everything that was part of my Virginia life where it should have been left: in Virginia. Including barbecuing as an excuse to socialize. Maybe that will end, now that I own HAL-9000.

As I sat there the first evening I used my new grill, Budweiser in-hand, feet up on the railing of my deck, *The Marriage of Figaro* playing loudly on the stereo, Ten Mile Creek gurgling a stone's throw away, while Gay sat beside me reading, leaving the grill-operations to me, as well she should have, all this old life stuff is flashing through my mind for the first time in a very long time. I am half here, half somewhere else, a long time ago, and for once, that does not make me feel uncomfortable.

But, as I ask Gay how she wants her steak cooked (I've been married to this woman forever, I know how she likes her steak cooked, and it doesn't matter how she answers, or for that matter, that I already know how she will answer, because I have already managed to burn the steaks through-and-through by the time the question surfaces), I know one thing for certain, as much as I have ever known any one thing in my life: spring has come at long last to the High Country. The time for seasonal rebirth is well-nigh upon this splendid mountain-dominated land.

Now all I need is a package of hot dogs and an ice-cream maker and maybe even a few of my old Virginia buddies.

Or, is that taking all this too far?

Peace on Dirt? Maybe, Maybe Not

It is mid-May and, as some of the snow finally begins to recede at the base of "my trail" (it will be at least six weeks before the upper reaches, at 12,000 feet, are snow-free), I swear, this year things will be different. I swear.

Some preliminary explanation is in order here. First of all, the trail in question, an eight-mile stretch of the Colorado Trail that runs through the heart of Summit County, is not actually mine. I have, however, adopted every inch of those eight miles, through the Colorado Trail Foundation's Adopt-a-Trail program and, when you hike several hours into the heart of the steep and rugged Ten Mile Range with all manner of trail-repairing tools on your back every three weeks or so from June till November, you get feeling a tad possessive.

"My trail" actually belongs to all the people of this fine country, and it is administered on their behalf by the Dillon Ranger District of the Arapaho National Forest. I knew when I first volunteered to adopt my section of the CT that there was a very good chance some on-trail inter-personal problems could result. As I live only about five miles from the trailhead, I had hiked my now-adopted section at least a dozen times before being offered the opportunity to become a blood brother with it. Therefore, I knew full well that I was adopting a multiple-use section of trail, where hikers make up the minority of users.

Far and away, the most use on my trail in the non-snow months comes from mountain bikers, which I do not particularly mind, because mountain biking is at least a self-propelled sport. Whatever extra erosional damage mountain bikes may cause on my trail (and they do cause some), I am only too happy to help fix. But, ATVers and dirt bikers are also more than welcome, legally, on my trail, which connects Gold Hill Trailhead, just north of Breckenridge, with the crest of the Ten Mile Range, just east of, and several thousand feet above, Copper Mountain Resort. And ATVers and dirt bikers I do particularly mind using my trail on many different levels.

For a number of reasons, mine is not the best stretch of the CT. Far from it. Not only is it located in one of the busiest tourist counties in the Rockies and, therefore, sees way too much use, but, at the same time, the forest through which it passes is decidedly unhealthy. This is a mono-growth lodgepole pine woods that is badly in need of a huge, monster fire—a reality that makes the local tourist-industry powers that be want to pull what little hair they have left out.

But, the worst part of my trail is the fact that near-bouts any mode of transportation is welcome on it. If someone wanted to drive a tank from Gold Hill to Copper, they could probably do it. This means my trail is, in many places, torn up all to hell. It also means that the quiet backcountry aesthetics of the trail can be terminated in a skinny minute by a line of stinky, loud ATVs being driven by fat Texans.

But, as I said, I knew beforehand about all these things and vowed, once the adoption papers were signed, sealed, and delivered, to keep a smile on my face, no matter who or what I ran into on my trail. The local mountain bike community hereabouts, which is substantial, has, of late, been bending over backwards, by and large, to manifest the attitude articulated by the bumper sticker slogan, "Peace on Dirt," and I swore to ten or twelve deities that, as I maintained my trail, I would adopt that slogan as my personal motto.

Well, that attitude didn't even last until I was done with my very first Adopt-a-Trail-oriented foray along those eight miles. My wife and I were doing a basic reconnaissance hike, trying to ascertain just how much work adopting a stretch of trail would actually entail. Suddenly, we came across three motorcycle helmets laying seemingly abandoned alongside the trail. We were perplexed, until we heard, off in the distance, in an alpine meadow, the unmistakable whine of two-stroke engines revving time and time again up towards the redline, just below the tree line. A few minutes later, three four-wheeled ATVs appeared. The riders, who, along with their hideous machines, were covered top-to-bottom with mud that, scant seconds before, was anchoring plant life in the aforesaid meadow, were coming to retrieve their helmets. I flew into a stuttering rage, yelling about how four-wheeled vehicles weren't allowed on that particular stretch of trail (I was sort of stretching the truth on that one, hoping to make my newfound enemies feel like criminals, which, in my opinion, they sorta were), and even if they were allowed, they shouldn't be, and even if they should be, that's no excuse to leave the trail with the express purpose of tearing up alpine meadows.

As my face was getting redder and redder, the ATVers remained remarkably calm, almost indifferent. Suddenly, one of them made an obscene gesture towards me and called me a "Nature Nazi." Before I could compose myself enough to (1) start swinging my hiking stick at his face and (2) realize that was a compliment, they tore off down the trail, laughing.

I decided right then and there to sprint to the closest mountain bike store to buy one of those "Peace on Dirt" bumper stickers, just so I could tear it up and stomp it into the very dirt upon which I was being admonished to be peaceful. If I was going to be a Nature Nazi, by gods, I was going to be the Heinrich Himmler of the backcountry.

Within one week of adopting my trail, I rapidly found myself becoming the Curmudgeonous Ogre of the Rockies. Peace On Dirt, my ass. My backcountry demeanor changed toward the severely negative with that one ATV interaction.

For the next few months, if I saw a mountain biker tearing down my trail while it was muddy, I would jump down his or her throat. And woe be unto the poor soul who dropped so much as a gum wrapper on my trail within eye-shot of yours truly. And, if I saw an ATVer or a dirt biker, even if they were doing nothing technically wrong, I would stand in the middle of my trail with my hand out like an elementary school crossing guard and inform the lazy SOBs that they were, well, lazy SOBs, and that if they had anything going for them at all as sentient beings, they would repent their evil ATVing and dirt-biking ways and immediately push their foul vehicles off the closest cliff (of which there are many to choose from) and start walking up toward the summit of the closest mountain, even if it killed them, which hopefully it would.

And, I must admit, for the first month or so, I felt much better having opted for the *No* Peace on Dirt Unless It's on My Terms credo. It was like adopting an eight-mile stretch of trail helped unlock the real me. I even took my curmudgeon role on the road, deciding that limiting such a liberating attitude to one short section of trail in one's home county was a waste of good and beneficial surliness.

Of course, when I was back on my trail, there was still this nagging little problem about legal uses. It's hard to make a valid backcountry point to a non-hiking transgressor when it, generally, is not a valid point even slightly. In the eyes of the law, I simply had no right to give people a ration of grief while they were out in the woods having a good and sadly legal time.

That dilemma got me thinking about my options. In order to make this little piece of the world a better place, I could work to get the Forest Service to close down my trail to all but the most saintly of uses, which, in my mind, consist of walking and resting during one's hike. And/or I could petition the Colorado Trail Foundation to alter the CT's route, so it goes places where ATVs and dirt bikes are disallowed.

But, I suspect neither option would achieve anything, at least not for many years. So, I finally had to admit to myself, as the summer was fast winding down, that I would have to shoot and kill every ATVer and dirt biker on earth, if there was any chance whatsoever of achieving peace on my little stretch of dirt. Okay, so that's not what I really decided, though the thought did enter my head.

What I really decided was that I was stuck with a section of trail where ATVs and dirt bikes were flat-out allowed, end of story. Meaning I could continue to vent my spleen on my trail every fifteen seconds or so to poor, unsuspecting schmucks and schmuck-ettes on vacation, or I could work hard (well, semi-hard) towards modifying my on-trail attitude, for the sake of mitigating an ever-more-prominent hypertension problem. The only other choice I could see was to de-adopt my trail, and that was really no choice at all.

During the following winter, one of my closest amigos tactfully brought it to my attention that the confrontational backcountry attitude I had developed and fine-tuned the prior summer had, on numerous occasions, embarrassed several of my hiking companions, who either did not fully share that attitude or, if they did, preferred not to articulate it at 190 decibels every half-mile. And I had to admit that my curmudgeon-of-the-trail persona was beginning to effect my own backcountry experiences. It was like I now entered the woods not so much to enjoy the experience of nature but, rather, to experience the joy of confrontation. I would hit the trail with the same attitude I take with me to martial arts tournaments. I was clearly losing something very important to my sanity. My buddy and I ended up talking about this use-conflict-in-the-backcountry thing a lot, generally while we were cross-country skiing in areas where snowmobilers are allowed.

While I would turn red-in-the-face at the mere sound of some distant snowmobile, my friend would always stay mellow, even when an interminable line of those God-awful stink-sleds passed within two feet of us. He would wave and ask how everyone is doing and say what a nice day it was, even if it was twenty-below and gray and snowing nasty-like. And, while I often thought of my buddy as a backcountry wimp, it was becoming increasingly obvious that he was enjoying his outdoor trips a lot more than I was.

My friend continues to insist that, with limited exceptions, such as drunk hunters and bank robbers escaping on-foot through the woods, outdoor enthusiasts, no matter their preferred mode of travel, have, if nothing else, the outdoors in common. And my friend feels that commonality very well has the potential of bridging other, nonoutdoors-issue gaps. He believes that, with something as awesome and important as a love of the backcountry in common, we ought to be able to get along, at least on a basic level and, if outdoorspeople of different stripes cannot get along, or at least communicate non-negatively, while out on the trail, then there is likely very little hope for mankind to solve its off-trail problems, like war, famine, ozone depletion, and the proliferation of American fast-food outlets in foreign countries.

Now, my friend does not take his argument to an absurd extreme. He feels it is perfectly justifiable to become irked with people who blatantly disregard fundamental backcountry ethics, whether that blatant disregard stems from ignorance or malice. And he feels it is equally justifiable to bring one's irkedness to the attention of the offending boobs, in whatever tone of voice is necessary to make the point, when they are partaking in inappropriate backcountry behavior. He just doesn't happen to think that on-trail, use-oriented confrontations ought to take place as a matter of natural course, like a reflex motion when a doctor whacks the crud out of your knee with a rubber hammer.

I have taken that argument to heart throughout the long High Country winter. As a result, I have forced myself several times to actually not spit and scowl the exact moment a snowmobile passed me while I was skiing along the Shrine Pass Road (where snowmobiles are, sadly to say, perfectly legal). I have even thought about enlisting the help of local ATVers and dirt bikers to help me maintain my trail.

While that attitude may seem like a cop-out to some, for me, it's a necessary evil (or maybe a necessary good)—one that is worth adopting, or at least test-driving for a while.

And, if it doesn't work out, if I cannot overcome my natural tendency to be confrontational on the trail with people like ATVers and dirt bikers, there's always the Curmudgeonous Ogre of the Rockies character, just waiting for an encore appearance. There are worse roles to play.

A County of Death

When I tell people about what life is like in the High Country, interspliced with the concepts of amalgamated culture, multi-generational socio-economic layering (whatever the hell that is), and partying till you puke, I have to include one somber note. Those of us who dwell up here all have to deal with death as though it were a roommate, a hiking partner, a lover.

Not only do we all have to deal with death the way every other sentient being has to deal with death—that is to say, all of our butts are going to venture forth to hobnob with the Grim Reaper one of these days—but, at the same time, we have to deal with the reality that, for a county with a mere 14,000 full-time residents, we have a disproportionate number of folks meeting their maker hereabouts on a nearbouts weekly basis.

Sometimes, it seems like we are cursed. Certainly, the number of deaths in Summit County might seem particularly high for someone, such as yours truly, who works for a daily newspaper, where information about every death in the county eventually comes. But, there are absolutes to balance journalistic impressions. Though I forget the exact number, last year we had something like thirty deaths here, and only one or two were from natural causes.

I read a story recently about how Lake City, Colorado, had its first resident death in something like a billion years. In Summit County, that thought is as foreign as it is in Denver's high-crime Capitol Hill neighborhood. That the amount of death in Summit County testifies to how hard and (hopefully) wonderfully we and the people who visit us live rarely makes it any easier to deal with. Sure, we can all talk bravely—and we should talk bravely—about how so-and-so died doing the thing he or she loved best (skiing, mountaineering, ice-climbing, kayaking, partying till he/she puked). We can say how so-and-so would have rather died in the High Country than anywhere else on Earth.

We can say all these kinds of things, but the truth is, man oh man, for a rural county landlocked in the heart of the Rockies, we must steel ourselves towards death in ways generally reserved for members of the military or police forces.

Saturday afternoon, several of us were sitting on the deck at Golden Annie's sipping cold ones when the Flight for Life helicopter took off from the Summit Medical Center in Frisco. We silently watched it make its way west. When it was out of sight, we talked for at least ten minutes about Flight for Life and its astounding importance to this community. I told everyone theregathered about the time I saw the Flight for Life helicopter land over near Officer's Gulch. A Breckenridge man, Newt Whatley, had been buried by an avalanche while ice-climbing. It was just about dusk, and everyone was standing around the side of the interstate, shivering. It was a time when all of us knew on a visceral level that Newt probably would not make it. He had been buried too long.

The Flight for Life helicopter landed on the bike path in what seemed like highly improbable circumstances. The wind was blowing, and the landing site was very narrow. The slightest mishap could have been devastating. But, land it did and, when the Search and Rescue team finally and valiantly got Newt out, that helicopter took off safely and flew to Denver like the wind. Yet, to no avail, because Newt died some hours later, though people said lesser men would have expired long before, without a fight.

I have no idea who was flying the Flight for Life helicopter that blustery winter day when Newt died. It might have been Gary McCall, or it might have been someone else. All I know now is that McCall was at the controls as the helicopter took off as we were sitting there drinking beer at Golden Annie's Saturday afternoon, and not long after, it crashed on the side of Huron Peak, a fourteener over in the Sawatch Range that my wife and I climbed last fall. A hiker had broken her ankle and needed rescuing. Flight for Life was—as it has been for the past twenty-something years—called.

McCall was killed, as was nurse Sandy Sigman of Denver. They are still trying to figure out what went wrong. Once again, death visited the Summit. It is hard to get away from death here.

When I ride my bike towards the bike path in Frisco, I pass by the spot where, last summer, I watched an astounding extrication operation performed by the Frisco Fire Department. A car had careened off an interstate overpass and landed on its top. The daughter and wife somehow survived; the husband was killed, his face completely crushed in. The scars on the road are still there. And they will be there until the road is re-paved.

That spot is less than fifty yards from my front door.

When I park my car at the Meadow Creek Trailhead to go hiking, which I do at least twenty times a year, I try not to let my eyes wander too far into the woods, at least until I am well up the hill towards Lilypad Lake. This is the area where Kelly Nugent's body was found last winter. Or, rather, parts of her body. By the time her remains were discovered, there was very little left to discover. She was a beautiful young lady last seen hitchhiking over from Leadville. I cannot stand the thought of stumbling upon her remains while I'm out for a pleasant stroll through the hills. Nor can I stand the thought of how she might have died. I do not want this sort of mortal contamination here in this lovely place.

Yet, it is here.

I drink often in the Moose Jaw, and every time I hoist my first drink in there, I silently toast Todd Freese, late son of the owner, Linda Colety. Todd passed away near Christmas a couple of years ago, and it was a bitter pill to swallow for the entire community. It's hard to not think of him when you're in the Jaw, yet there is no way not to.

Sometimes people frame the context of life in terms of death. When I drive to Breckenridge, I think often of Laura Smith, who died last year while I was on vacation in New Mexico. I got the word when I returned home, sun-tanned and well-rested. The word deflated me. Death was here yet again. Laura was driving too fast and had had too much to drink and failed to negotiate a severe corner.

I did not know her well. Many of my closest friends did. For several days, many of the people I know and love best were having trouble breathing.

It has gotten to the point where our High Country landscape is defined by who died where, when, and how.

As these words are being written, my wife, along with myriad family members, is hiking in the Sawatch, near Huron. Most of the time when Gay hikes, I am near her and, sadly and stupidly, I operate under the assumption that death will not take her as long as I am in close proximity. If anything bad happens, I will either save her or death will take me instead.

Whenever she is out in the woods alone, my attention is diverted, until I see her pull up in her Subaru. Then I can finally relax. This is not a sexist thing; it's not that I believe that, because she is a woman, she cannot take care of herself in the mountains. It is, rather, a community-of-man thing that, in this case, manifests itself as a spousal thing. She always breathes a sigh of relief when I pull up safely in my Jeep, too.

I was asked by a basically sedentary sister-in-law the other day why we (in her question, she was asking about Gay and me) "do" the things we do. She has heard enough in the way of hare-brained near-miss stories from us over the years that she has given thought to this subject. She wanted to know why we would risk the danger of (in this case) taking a one-hundred-mile hike that's almost entirely above tree line that we have scheduled for later this month down in the San Juans.

I pondered her question in the context of not Gay and I, but, rather "we"—the people like us who call the High Country home for a big ol' set of reasons that most often have little or nothing to do with making a living in the traditional sense. Why do we aggressively stare the angel of death in the eye so often—especially when we know full well that, by so doing, we so often make that angel take flight, if not towards us, then towards someone else.

My sister-in-law was halfway smiling when she asked the question, and knowing that we have just had a Flight for Life helicopter go down with two fatalities the day before this question was asked and that we are still mourning those fourteen valiant firefighters who died near Glenwood Springs, I had to tell her that we could not even consider living any other way. At least I don't think so.

And that's what makes High Country dwellers so special. It's not that we court death; it's rather that we do not, as a matter of course, let the notion of our own imminent mortality get in the way of life. I told a friend recently that, in most of the country, by the time people are my age, they have already stopped living. But not up here. By the time people are my age (thirty-eight, for the record) in the High Country, we're only just getting started. Each place I would hope has something sociologically that makes it special. That attitude is one of the things that makes the people who live up here where the air is thin and clean special.

We are not cursed here in the Summit: we are blessed . . . by life. And that, of course, has its price.

At least here, the angel of death will never die from boredom.

Epilogue: Higher

My wife, Gay, and I were driving along the dirt road that connects Shrine Pass with the little town of Redcliff the other evening. It was the first day of October. We were on our way to a housewarming party that would be attended by the vast majority of the close friends we have made in our time living up here in the High Country.

It was dusk, we had already had a few beers and were having a few more, and we were bounding along in my Jeep, Worf, at what was, in retrospect, probably not a prudent speed. We were listening to a Nancy Griffith tape at a reasonable volume and basically just shooting the breeze, not only spouse-to-spouse style, but best-friend-to-best-friend style.

Gay was hobnobbing about her most recent photographic forays (she had been working particularly hard trying to capture the High Country fall on film), while I was talking about my upcoming writing projects, which, as usual, seemed overwhelming to an absurd degree.

Suddenly, for reasons that probably had as much to do with beer intake as anything else, I started to enter near-weepiness. My stereotypically male emotional system went, embarrassingly enough, into a rare, teary-eyed overdrive. Usually, when I suffer from a bout of emotionalism, it manifests itself by way of side-splitting laughter or red-eyed rage.

For about the billionth time since I moved to the High Country, I simply could not believe what a lucky hombre I was and am, and my happiness, in this instance, caused me to choke up, making it so I had to swig my beer at a slower rate than normal.

I mean, here I was with my honey, a huge can of Foster's resting comfortably in my lap, driving Worf down one of the loveliest dirt roads in the state on my way to visit several of my very best friends at dusk during aspen season while listening to one of my favorite singers.

Shit don't get much better than that.

The season was to the point that it was no longer a full season, but rather, a season-in-decline. Though there were still golden leaves galore, at least half of the aspens on the hillsides along the road stood stark naked, stoically waiting for the onslaught of winter, which could have kicked in at any moment. When I pulled over in the gathering darkness to take a leak, it was chilly enough that I pulled a pile sweatshirt on. I could see my breath in the dim light. The woods were silent, most of the birds having smartly flown the coop for the season.

It really hit me as I stood there relieving myself: there is nowhere else on Earth I could imagine living. The High Country is my own personal version of paradise. Yes, it is cold as crap most of the time. Housing prices are off the scale. It takes an hour to buy a pack of cigars at Safeway sometimes because of the long lines of tourists that overrun my home town most of the year. The place is thick with real estate and developer invertebrates who are, their marketing pabulum notwithstanding, more concerned with milking the High Country for big bucks than they are with maintaining any of the "lifestyle" stuff they always blab on about.

Yes, there are battles to be fought in the High Country—but this is one of the few places I have ever lived that is worth fighting for, worth calling people names and cussing them out in public in front of their children and, every once in a good while, firing up the chain saw for a little nighttime custom work on developments-in-progress

And, though Gay and I have talked a lot not so much about moving away from the High Country as we have about "checking someplace else out for a while" (the Eastern Shore of Virginia and the Gulf Coast of Texas have come up more than once), we have essentially, without speaking the words, come to understand that this wonderful part of the world is not only where we live, but home.

Home sweet home.

And, as such, being lifelong renters, we have started looking around to buy a place that will likely serve as the Fayhee bar, grille, and flophouse for the next however many number of years. Though we love Summit County to death on just about all levels, it's starting to get a tad crowded here, and as I have indicated, you can't throw a rock without hitting a realtor or a developer, which on the one hand is good, but on the other hand is not so good.

So, I have finally talked Gay into considering moving to Leadville. At 10,300 feet above sea level, it's the highest-altitude city in North America (Alma, at 10,400 feet, is the highest-altitude town). That's 1,200 feet higher than we already live—with a perfect view of the two tallest peaks in the Rockies, to boot.

There are few domicile-related things that could possibly make me happier than I already am here in the heart of the Rockies. And one of those is moving even higher, because, you know, high is cool, and higher is cooler.

About the Author

M. John Fayhee is a long-time contributing editor to *Backpacker* magazine and a veteran outdoor writer who has written for *Sports Illustrated, Outside, Sierra, Islands, Adventure Travel, Summit,* and *Canoe.* Fayhee is also the author of *Mexico's Copper Canyon Country,* published by Johnson Books, and *Along the Colorado Trail,* published by Westcliffe. He is currently working on a book about his experiences in the world of martial arts.

Fayhee lives at an elevation of 9,100 feet with his wife, Gay Gangel-Fayhee, in Summit County, Colorado, where he works as an editor/writer for the *Summit Daily News.*